The Cool Girl's Guide to Crochet

Nicki Trench

The Cool Girl's Guide to Crochet

Nicki Trench

Everything the novice crocheter needs to know

This is a Parragon Publishing Book
This edition published in 2006

Parragon Publishing
Queen Street House
4 Queen Street
Bath BA1 1HE, UK

ISBN 1-40548-345-8

The author would like to thank the following people without whom the book would
have been a lot less fun to write:

Pattern designers: Sian Brown, Annalisa Dunne, Joey Griffiths, Vikki Haffenden, Beryl
Oakes, Amy Phipps, Zara Poole, Nikki Ryan, Rebecca Smith and Emmaline Woodman
Models: Camilla Perkins and Rebecca Hawes
Stylist: Sue Lee
Also thanks to: David, Maddy, Roger, Sue and the Cowans

For Butler and Tanner
Project editor: Julian Flanders
Copy editor: Emma Clegg
Designer: Carole McDonald
Pattern checker: Margaret O'Mara

Location and techniques photography: Carole McDonald
Artworks: Sue Lee

Additional photos provided by: page 8 Rowan Yarns, page 38 left: Piku of Finland,
www.piku.fi., middle: Colinette Yarns, right: Mary-Helen.

Printed in China

Contents

PART ONE

New-Age Crochet

Crochet's back in the limelight

Crochet is losing its old-fashioned reputation. You may associate the craft with black-clad grannies of southern Europe sitting in their doorways in the evening sunshine, adeptly crocheting doilies on which to put their candlesticks. Yet now, with the increasing demand for hand-crafted accessories and domestic items, crochet is re-inventing itself for the 21st century.

Crochet on the Rowan stand at the Knitting and Stiching Show, London.

Reinventing crochet

In the year 2000 Rowan Yarns, realizing that there was a younger market who were coming back to crafts, brought out an exciting new range of thick superchunky yarn called Big Wool and Biggy Print. Their range of stylish mini-books, full of stunning fashion photography, helped stimulate knitting and crochet as popular crafts. Yarns from breeds of sheep such as the merino with an ultra-soft fleece are being mixed with real luxury fibers from breeds such as alpaca, cashmere, and angora to create new and versatile yarns. So shades of yarn are no longer defined by shiny acrylics in primary colors.

In the USA crochet is more popular than knitting, 80-90 per cent of people who crochet make afghan blankets; they are usually made from squares that are joined together, so it feels as if you have achieved something in a short space of time and they are easy to make. Most people who crochet also tend to knit, the two crafts go hand in hand.

In the UK knitting still dominates over crochet, although British yarn companies are now incorporating crochet patterns into their knitting pattern books. British yarn company Rowan, has recently added 'crochet' to the titles of their popular magazines and the titles now read 'Knitting and Crochet patterns' instead of just 'Knitting patterns'.

Designs for garments tend to be knitted or a combination of both knitting and crochet. Knitting is generally a tighter fabric and crochet a little more open and best suited to fashion and home accessories such as scarves, hats, blankets, bags, cushion covers, and is also often used as an attractive edging for a knitted piece.

People are turning back to home crafts as an antidote to a harsh computerized world. Career women are now reclaiming their domestic heritage. By day they strike lucrative deals: they are well-educated, smart and everything the feminists of the 1960s dreamed of. By night, after a long day at the office, the career woman throws on her apron, bakes homemade muffins and runs along to her local knitting and crochet club.

In spite of the march of Ikea-style minimalism, chintz and gingham never go out of fashion, forming part of a security blanket that we all need. Whatever their lifestyle choice, women won't abandon their natural nesting instincts. In the USA Tupperware-style parties are making a comeback and knitting and crochet clubs are having the same impact. Housewives, working moms, single women, and career women are getting together to rediscover this ancient bond. They meet in each other's homes, in cafés and fashionable bars to wind down and relax with a glass of wine or

Rowan Slingbag

a hot chocolate. These women may well be able to afford luxury knitting items, but prefer the pleasure of knitting or crocheting their own.

In the USA Stitch 'n' Bitch groups have been set up throughout the country. The craze was started by Debbie Stoller, the well-known author and journalist, who sees knitting and crochet as a representation of a new age of feminism. Mostly, though, women join the groups for the social scene rather than for any strong political motivation. They meet, chat, and swap patterns and yarn. It seems that with family groups being more scattered, women turn to hobby groups to form their own community networks.

The increasing popularity of humble, home-making activities such as knitting and crochet is linked to the fact that we live in more uncertain times. People are turning to their homes, places where they feel safe, and where the smell of freshly baked bread, floral interiors and the sound of clicking needles gives comfort from the disturbing images filtered into our homes by the media.

Who crochets?

Anybody interested in creative, individual work will be interested in crochet. On the back of the home do-it-yourself revolution, people are making quick and easy projects that fit with modern-day items. There is a huge trend in wearing anything that is homemade. Bored with designer fashions, people are looking for items that make them stand out in a crowd and at a fraction of the price of couture-house and catwalk styles. In the stores, too, you'll find crochet everywhere, particularly crocheted accessories, such as hats, bags, scarves and the ever-present poncho. There are even crocheted thongs and shoes.

Men who crochet

In the USA men crochet and nobody bats an eyelid. It has become perfectly acceptable to sit next to a man in the subway, or in a bar, who is crocheting something for his wife. It even seems to be a good way of attracting women if you're single - a woman always likes a sensitive type and crochet is a very tactile craft. You are, however, less likely to find a man crocheting in the UK, where crochet is still a mainly female pastime. In the USA, there is an online yahoo group, Men Who Crochet, which has it's own podcast crochet show that broadcasts every week with news, tips and general crochet chat. This can be either listened to on the Internet or downloaded onto your MP3 player. It seems that crochet has a mathematical element to it which suits the male brain, and the rhythmic craft has attracted even the butchest men, such as Ian Johnson from Boise State Broncos football team in Idaho, who crochets and sells team hats for his fellow players and fans. His nickname is "Crochet boy." "How can you tease a guy if he's making stuff for you?," one of his teammates said.

Crochet in fashion

Crochet is now scattered all over the catwalks and every one of the big fashion houses seems to have crochet in some form in their collection. Just flick through *Vogue* and *Elle* and you'll find pages with crochet everywhere. There is an exhibition in Italy called *Pitti Filati*, that takes place every season, to show current and future trends in knitwear, which has been packed with buyers from Prada, Louis Vuitton, and Stella McCartney, who are all using hand knitting and crochet in their collections.

Celebrity crocheters

Even celebrities are taking up knitting and crochet. The combination of having extended gaps between shoots or recording sessions and crochet being such a portable craft makes it seem an ideal way to pass the time. Celebrities such as Julia Roberts, Vanna White, Rosie Perez, Madonna, and Sarah Jessica Parker have all been spotted proudly with hook and yarn between their fingers.

It is a well-known fact that E.M. Forster, author of *Howards End*, *A Room with a View*, and *A Passage to India*, became totally hooked on crochet in the 1930s. So you are in good company.

Seung Hee Lee

What is crochet?

Simple crochet

Crochet is a series of knots intertwined with a hook that make a piece of knotted textile. A succession of loops are pulled through each other to make an intricate, yet beautiful piece of fabric.

Any lengths of textile can be used to crochet. Traditionally cotton was used for intricate lace work, but now thicker, chunkier yarns are more commonly used to create fashionable bags, accessories, and garments. String, rag, or leather can also be used. You will often find a beautiful bag or summer hat crocheted in the kind of twine that can easily be bought from your local hardware store.

Crochet is so much easier than knitting. There are only three basic stitches, with others just variations of those three. Often children are taught crochet before knitting–it's a lot less daunting to just have one short hook and it's easier to navigate than using needles. Best of all, if you make a mistake with crochet you can just take out the hook and pull the work back to the previous stitch and only have one stitch to pick up again, instead of a whole mound of stitches on a knitting needle.

Crochet projects are easy to carry around, so you can crochet anywhere–on trains, planes, and automobiles (though not when you're driving!). It is a very rhythmic action and can be quite mesmerizing to watch. Most crochet projects are quite small. Large garments tend to be knitted rather than crocheted and the other big items such as afghan blankets tend to be made up of small crocheted squares joined together.

Filet Crochet

This type of crochet is popular with those who want to create a design on an item. This is a technique based on a simple network with a regular, square grid made up of double and chain stitches. Patterns are shown in the form of a squared chart. The patterns can have very intricate designs: flowers, geometric patterns, lettering and sometimes even whole scenes.

Afghan crochet

This is a particular type of crochet that is worked back and forth without turning the work. Afghan crochet is worked with a longer hook than the normal crochet hook, it's required to hold loops that are made on the first half of the row before working them off on the second half of the row. Afghan crochet makes a very dense fabric.

Crochet in art

Textile arts are now becoming tremendously popular. There was recently a show called Not the Knitting You Know at the Eleven Eleven Sculpture Space in Washington DC, featuring some stunning sculptures using both knitting and crochet.

Crochet is ideally suited as an art form; it produces big loops and can easily create a sense of texture and design.

Git-Ying Tse

There are specific crochet artists who are exhibiting their work throughout the world. It seems the popularity of textiles is continuing to expand with the university and college intake of textile graduates showing a dramatic rise in recent years.

Freeform crochet

This is a unique way of self expression in the craft, where the crocheted fabric takes on a life of its own. The technique of freeform crochet is used to create a piece of crocheted artwork. Structures are in two and three dimensions and the piece is made using different yarns and textiles to create a beautiful individual piece of art.

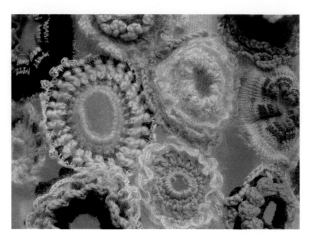

Detail from green sweater, Seung Hee Lee

1950s

New-Age Crochet

Crochet quiz

Now you've read a little bit about the subject, try our crochet quiz for fun. Don't let the clues put you off; the answers are in your crochet knowledge and are commonly used crochet terms.

1. What traditional crochet item stops your vases from scratching your polished tables?

2. What looks like a musical note but has more to do with hooks and loops?

3. Which sheep has an extremely soft fleece and likes to dance the flamenco?

4. What does Peter Pan's arch-enemy use for one-handed crochet?

5. Which useful instruction shows the way to sail or a patient's progress?

6. Who knows which Peruvian animal this is?

7. What do shy actors use for nude scenes or dangerous stunts?

8. What do you have to do to get your boat gently down the stream?

9. Which old-fashioned tale may be called that because the teller can spin it out?

10. What sharp pain do you get if you run too fast after sitting and crocheting for a long while?

11. Boys with high voices. Maybe three of them?

12. What isn't round and has four equal sides?

13. Matisse was fond of them and they are an essential instruction?

14. What many hands do on New Year's Eve?

15. What major brand of yarns and patterns produces the popular superchunky yarns: Biggy Print and Big Wool?

16. Contrary to the flat earth theory, what shape is the planet Earth?

17. What's a bright and colorful cheerleader accessory?

18. What Dracula's title?

19. Something you might do on a banana skin?

20. What kind of gang is famous for its convictions?

Answers

1. Doilies	11. Treble
2. Crochet	12. Square
3. Merino	13. Patterns
4. Hook	14. Join
5. Chart	15. Rowan Yarns
6. Alpaca	16. Round
7. Double	17. Pom pom
8. Row	18. Count
9. Yarn	19. Slip
10. Stitch	20. Chain

PART TWO

What You Need...
...and What To Do With It

★ Yarn and thread

You can crochet with almost anything that takes the form of a long, continuous line, is reasonably flexible and can be put around a crochet hook. There are a lot of new yarns available with which to experiment. You can even use string, wire, leather or strips of fabric.

YARN TYPES

The many varieties of sumptuous yarn that are now available make crochet a delightful pastime. Luxury yarns such as alpaca, angora, cashmere, and mohair are being mixed with the soft fleece of the merino sheep (originally from Spain but now raised all over Europe, Australia, and the US). In the past woollen fabrics were often rough and itchy, but the new popularity of luxury yarns means that people are willing to pay more for their soft, sumptuous feel. Color palettes have also changed from the bright, luminescent colors that were typical of acrylic yarns to match the natural and subtle colors that people are now choosing for their home décor.

Wool

There are many types of wool sourced from different breeds of sheep and there are, in turn, many types of fleece with varying levels of softness. Having become accustomed to the comfort that was introduced by the use of manmade fibers, consumers are now demanding softer, natural wool, in an abundance of different thicknesses, from fine 4 plys to superchunky thick yarns that come in a variety of plain and fancy textures.

Sheep breeds with fleeces that create fine wools include Delaine Merino, Shetland and Debouillet. In the UK the fleece of the Blue Leicester sheep is often mixed with other

less fine fleeces to provide the required softness. Medium wools include Dorset, Suffolk, Shropshire, and Navajo Churro; long wools include Lincoln, Cotswold, Teeswater, and Shetland. Coarse wools tend to be used for other functions such as carpets or wool insulation.

If you buy a woollen garment that has been hand knitted or crocheted in South America, it is sometimes rough on the skin and may even have bits of wood and straw tangled up in it that haven't been removed at the fleece combing stage; it seems the South Americans are less concerned with the roughness of some garments, maybe because they use these as jackets or outerwear and wear something else underneath. However, the alpaca is native to South America and has an incredibly soft and luscious fleece and is becoming more popular throughout the US and Europe as a hand knitting yarn.

Silk

One of the more expensive yarns with which to crochet, silk yarn is often mixed with wool, creating a distinctive sheen and a soft and silky feel. Silk creates a light and luxurious yarn that makes lovely summer wraps and tops. It feels very rich to the touch and is often worth the extra expense.

Cotton

Cotton is traditionally used for finer items such as doilies or lacy tablecloths. Double-knit cotton is a thicker cotton that is easy to crochet and can be useful for cushions or blankets and gives a thicker more plump feel than fine cotton. If you want a softer quality use wools or silky yarns.

Ribbon yarn

This yarn comes in all thicknesses and makes a very soft fabric. Light and cool, it is ideal for summer tops, cushions.

Eyelash yarn/hairy yarns

Although they have become popular in recent years, eyelash yarns are not ideally suited to crochet. This type of yarn tends to hide the stitch so it is difficult to see the stitch structure in the fabric. The hairs in the yarn also lock into each other making the loops awkward to pull through.

Fancy yarns

Any type of yarn that has been spun differently to form a curly or avant-garde look is called a fancy yarn. Some of these are spun with a mixture of fabric and wool to give an unusual effect.

String

A strong, firm material, string can look at home in any modern interior, particularly when used to crochet containers, runners and mats.

Rags

Use torn-up fabric to make rugs, bags, mats, or clothes.

Leather strips

With a glossy sheen, leather is very durable and can be effectively used for stylish interior accessories such as floor cushions or containers.

Raffia

A fun fabric for crocheting, raffia is the perfect material for making table mats and coasters. It comes in many colors as well as natural shades.

PLY

Yarn is available in the following thicknesses. When practising new crochet techniques, it is easier to avoid using fine yarns such as lurex and sport weight, the worsted weights and aran are ideal because they're easier to handle.

Fingering weight (or 4 ply)

An ideal yarn for light garments and one that is often used for baby clothes and summer tops.

Sport weight (or double knitting [dk])

Providing a good general thickness of yarn, sport weight yarn is easy to crochet with. It takes a medium-sized hook that is easy to handle and is useful for all kinds of projects.

Worsted weight (or aran)

Another yarn with a general application, worsted weight is thicker than double knitting and tends to be used for projects that require more warmth. Easy to handle, it is a good yarn for a beginner.

Chunky weight

Providing a warm, winter thickness of wool, a chunky yarn crochets quickly and is ideal for hats, scarves and gloves.

Extra-bulky weight (or superchunky)

The popularity of this thick yarn is largely responsible for the recent revival in knitting and crochet. An extra-bulky garment is generally crocheted with a super-thick-size hook. Perfect for those who want to crochet a hat or scarf in one evening.

★ How to read a label

Yarn labels contain all sorts of useful information. Although it's tempting to throw the label in the trash in your haste to get going on your crochet, you should definitely hold on to it for a while. You may, for example, run out of yarn and need an extra ball, in which case the label will tell you the exact dye-lot number and shade number you need–then you can get back to your supplier for an identical match.

The label gives washing and ironing instructions, vital for keeping your crochet in good condition. It also gives you the recommended gauge and needle sizes to suit the thickness of the yarn.

The basic information on the label will have the brand name, the type of yarn, such as sport (double knitting) or worsted (aran), and the name of the range, such as Cashmerino Aran.

★ Crochet equipment

Crochet is probably one of the most unencumbered crafts in terms of equipment. A small hook, a pair of sharp scissors, some yarn, and you'll be off to a good start.

HOOKS

Crochet hooks come in all sizes. Wool hooks start at around B/1 and go up to the superchunky size Q. The smaller sizes tend to be metal and as they get bigger they change to plastic. Wooden and bamboo hooks are available in the middle sizes and these have become popular in recent years. When buying bamboo hooks, it is wise to invest in quality brands to ensure the hook has a highly smooth finish. Most hooks will have a flat finger hold in the middle to help you achieve an even gauge.

Very tiny steel hooks are used for fine cotton threads–these can be size 14 or less. An Afghan hook is longer than a standard crochet hook and looks like a cross between a knitting needle and a crochet hook.

Different countries use different sizing units for hooks. The conversion chart to the right shows how the sizes convert from US sizes, to metric sizes, as well as the old UK sizes.

HOOK SIZE CONVERSION CHART

US	Metric	old UK
14 steel	0.60mm	–
12 steel	0.75mm	–
11 steel	1.00mm	–
8 steel	1.50mm	–
6 steel	1.75mm	–
B/1	2.00mm	14
C/2	2.50mm	12
D/3	3.00mm	10
E/4	3.50mm	9
F/5	4.00mm	8
G/6	4.50mm	7
H/8	5.00mm	6
I/9	5.50mm	5
J/10	6.00mm	4
–	6.50mm	3
K/10.5	7.00mm	2
L/11	8.00mm	–
M/13	9.00mm	–
N/15	10.00mm	–
O/P13	12.00mm	–
Q	15.00mm	–
S	20.00mm	–

PINS

Straight pins with colored ends should be used for blocking and checking gauge. Avoid ordinary pins with steel ends, which will get lost in the yarn. Safety pins are very useful for crochet; a small version of knitting stitch holders they are ideal for the small number of stitches used in crochet.

SCISSORS

Small scissors with sharp points are best as these allow you to isolate one strand of yarn for cutting at a time. Tie a piece of ribbon or yarn to the handle and tie the scissors on your knitting bag to avoid them getting lost.

WOOL SEWING NEEDLES

There are many different sizes of wool sewing needles. Buy those with a big enough eye through which to thread the yarn.

TAPE MEASURE

Use a cloth measure rather than the inflexible metal ones. Most have metric on one side and imperial on the other.

BUTTONS

Adding buttons is a really fantastic way to decorate and finish off a crocheted outfit, cushion or accessory. However, always choose your buttons wisely. A cheap unattractive button can undermine the quality of your garment. Make sure you choose the right size button for the buttonhole instructions in the pattern.

Buttons come in all shapes and sizes and are made from many different materials: ceramic, glass, plastic, shell, metal, wood, and horn. Check the washing instructions for the buttons as unprotected metal ones may rust.

Try making some crochet buttons (see page 37). These are simple to make and will match your garment perfectly.

★ Gauge

To make sure that you are working with the measurements that are instructed in the pattern you'll need to make a crocheted gauge square. By doing this you will be able to work out how tightly or loosely you make the crochet loops. This is because the size of the stitch will vary from person to person–almost everyone works with a different gauge. So if you don't work out your gauge before you start your pattern, your work may turn out bigger or smaller than you anticipated.

Most patterns follow the gauge rule that the stitch size is measured over an area of 4in (10cm) square, counting both rows and stitches.

1960s

Crochet through the decades

4 inch/10cm

4 inch/10cm

Gauge Square

To make a gauge square, create a piece of crochet approximately 5in (12.5cm) square using the recommended yarn and stitches in the pattern. Then count the number of rows and the number of stitches over a 4in (10cm) measurement. If these are consistent with the quoted dimensions for this measurement, then your gauge has matched the pattern, so you can then use the recommended hook size. If, however, you have more stitches in your square than stated you will need to change to a smaller sized hook. If you have too few stitches, you will need to change to a larger hook to achieve the correct gauge.

★ Crochet—first steps

The first stage of crochet is to find a way of holding the yarn and hook in a comfortable position so that the yarn slips through your fingers. You also need to get the right amount of gauge so that you can hold the yarn with your hook as it slips through the loops.

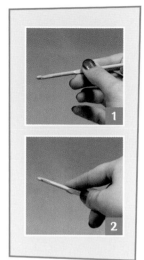

Holding the hook

There are two commonly used ways of holding the hook:

VERSION 1
Pick up the hook and hold it in the same way as a pen (1).

VERSION 2
Pick up the hook and hold it in the same way as a knife (2).

Holding the yarn

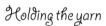

You need to hold the yarn so that it slips through your fingers. Here are two commonly used methods.

VERSION 1
Holding the yarn in your right hand, with your left-hand palm facing towards you, hook the yarn with your little finger (3). Turn your hand, catching the yarn with your index finger (4). Your left hand is now free to hold the yarn and hold the crocheted piece of fabric in place. Hold the crochet hook in the right hand (5).

VERSION 2
Holding the yarn in your right hand, with your left-hand palm facing towards you, hook the yarn over the little finger of your left hand, under the ring finger, and over the middle and second finger (6). Your left hand is now free to hold the yarn and hold the crocheted piece of fabric in place. Hold the crochet hook in the right hand (7).

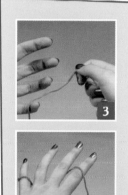

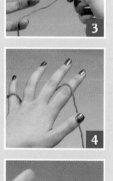

★ Stitches

Making the first loop

To make your first loop in crochet, you need to make a slip loop.

To do this, pick up your hook and position the yarn as explained on page 19. Make a loop with the end tail of the yarn (1). Let the tail end drop down over the back of the loop, catch the tail of the yarn with the hook and pull it through the loop (2). Hold the tail end and the ball end of the yarn in your left hand and tighten the loop with the hook in the opposite direction to create a stitch (3). Tighten the loop until it sits comfortably around the hook (4).

Chain (ch)

A chain is the basis of all crochet. It's used to begin a crochet pattern, at the beginning of a row and for lace patterns. Your crochet pattern will always tell you how many chains to make. Take care not to make the chains too tight and if you are a beginner be sure to practise your chain until you feel comfortable sliding the hook and yarn through each loop.

With your left hand hold the tail of the slip loop firmly (1). Catch the yarn with the hook and draw it through the loop (2). This makes your first chain. Make as many chains as indicated on the pattern (3). When counting the length of the chain, count each loop but not the one on the hook.

What You Need… and What To Do With It

Slip stitch (sl st)

This stitch is more commonly used to join the beginning of a round. If used row after row it creates a very dense, tight piece of fabric.

Make a chain (ch). Holding the end of the chain firmly, insert the hook through the second chain from the hook. Catch the yarn with the hook (a term called "wrap yarn over hook", abbreviated as yoh) and pull it through the chain and loop on the hook (1). This leaves one loop on the hook and completes the first slip stitch (sl st). Work the next slip stitch into the next chain in the same way. Continue working one sl st into each chain until you reach the end of the row. At the end of the row, turn your work, make one chain and continue back along the row in the same way.

Single crochet (sc)

Single crochet is the most common of all crochet stitches. This stitch creates a dense, hard-wearing fabric (see below).

ROW 1

Hold the smooth side of the chain facing you. From front to back, insert the hook through the second chain from the hook (1). There should be two loops on the hook. Wrap the yarn over the hook (yoh) and pull the yarn through two loops (2). This completes your first single crochet. You should now have one loop on the hook (3). Insert the hook into the next chain and continue until the end of the row, or as the pattern instructs.

ROW 2

When you get to the end of the row, turn your work so that your loop on the hook is at the right edge. In order to start the next row you then need to add a number of chain stitches called "turning chains." This will bring your work to the correct height for the next row.

For a single crochet you need one turning chain at the beginning of your row. Pull the loop through the loop on the hook to form a loose chain. This stitch is your first stitch and is counted as the first single crochet. Insert the hook into the next stitch and continue to work one sc into each stitch until the end of the row.

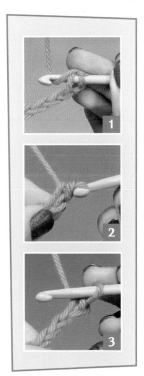

Double crochet (dc)

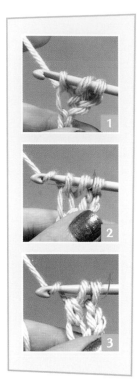

Double crochet is a taller stitch than single crochet. It also creates a lighter stitch (see below right). It is worked in the same way as a single crochet except the yarn is wrapped around the hook before beginning a stitch. The double crochet row always starts each row with three chains.

ROW 1

Begin the first row by working into the fourth chain from the hook. Wrap yarn over hook (yoh) and draw the yarn through the chain. There are now three loops around the hook (1). Wrap the yarn over the hook and draw yarn through the first two loops on the hook (2). Wrap the yarn around the hook and draw the yarn through the remaining two loops on the hook (3). One loop then remains on the hook. Work a double crochet into each stitch to the end. Turn and make three turning chains (ch). Work the first double crochet into the top of the next stitch.

Half double crochet (hdc)

A half double crochet is slightly shorter than a double crochet. It is made in a similar way to a single crochet, but with an extra twist of yarn.

Make a length of chains (ch). Wrap the yarn over the hook (yoh) and insert the hook into the third chain from the hook. Draw the yarn through the first loop, leaving three loops on the hook (1). Wrap the yarn over the hook (yoh) again and draw through all three loops on the hook (2).

Treble (tr)

Make a length of chains (ch). Wrap the
yarn twice over the hook (1), insert
the hook in the fifth chain from the hook.
Draw the loop through the chain. You
now have four loops on the hook (2).
Wrap the yarn again and draw through
the first two loops (3). Wrap the yarn
again (yoh) and draw through the next
two loops (4). Wrap the yarn again (yoh)
and draw through the last two loops,
leaving one loop on the hook (5).

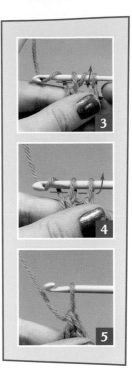

★ Stitch variations

Most stitches are variations of the basic stitches. Once
you've practised on a couple of easy projects, moving on
to a variation is easy.

Working into a chain space (ch sp)

Insert the hook into the space between the
stitches (1).

Double crochet cluster (dc cl)

A cluster is a group of stitches that are joined
closely together to give a particular shape.
To make a three-double crochet cluster (3dc
cl) use the instructions that follow.

Wrap the yarn over the hook (yoh),
insert the hook into the stitch, yoh and
draw through to the front, yoh and draw
through two loops (two loops remain on

the hook) (2). Yoh, insert hook into the
next stitch, draw through to the front
(yoh) and draw through two loops (three
loops remain on the hook) (3). Repeat step
2. There will now be four loops remaining
on the hook (4). Yrh and pull through all
four loops (5). This completes your three
double crochet cluster (3dc cl).

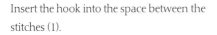

Popcorn

A variation of a cluster, a popcorn is a group of complete stitches worked into the same place, which is then folded and closed at the top. The number of stitches often varies and will be specified in the pattern. The instructions that follow show how to make a four-double crochet popcorn.

Make four double crochet stitches (dc) into the same place (1). Slip the last loop off the hook and reinsert the hook under the top two loops of the first dc in the group just made and pick up the loop that you took off the hook (2). Pull the loop through to close up the group of stitches (3).

1970s

Crochet through the decades

★ Basic techniques

Working in rows

Having finished your chains (ch), you can then begin working in rows. Begin the first row by inserting the hook in either the first, second, third, fourth or fifth chain, depending on the height of the stitch you are using. For example, when working with double crochet (dc) you need to make three more chains than required in the foundation row and then make the first stitch into the third chain from the hook (1).

This requirement will usually be explained in the pattern. Every following row will begin by using a "turning chain" (see below) which will bring the stitches up to the height of the stitch you are using and will be counted as your first stitch. The requirements of more complicated stitch patterns vary and will always be instructed in the crochet pattern.

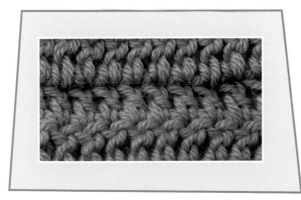

TABLE OF TURNING CHAINS

Single crochet (sc)	1 chain
Half double crochet (hdc)	2 chains
Double crochet (dc)	3 chains
Treble (tr)	4 chains
Double treble (dtr)	5 chains

Turning the work

When the first row is complete, you will need to turn the work. The trick to keeping a neat edge is to keep the direction you turn in consistent, either clockwise or counter-clockwise.

Working in rounds

One of the pleasures of crochet is that you can create circular constructions without any joining requirements. The basic technique of working in rounds is almost always the same. The thickness of the yarn will determine how many chains you need to make. Your pattern will instruct. To avoid creating too large a hole in the middle of the crochet, you'll usually be instructed to make four or six chains. The sequence that follows starts with six chains. Having created six chains (ch), insert the hook through the first chain. Wrap the yarn over the hook (yoh) and pull the loop through the chain and the loop on the hook (slip stitch). This will make a ring of chains (1). The next stage is usually to work a single crochet (sc) into the ring. Make one chain (2). Then insert the hook into the ring (not into the chain stitch), and make as many single crochets (sc) as the pattern instructs (3).

Marking the round when making spirals

When crocheting in circles you need to make a mark so you know when you've finished your row–otherwise you'll keep going round and round and not know what stage you have reached on your pattern.

Take a short length of yarn in a different color to your work. Place it over your crochet from front to back, under and to the left of the yarn (1). The yarn will be caught in position under the top of the first stitch. At the end of the round, pull it out and place in position for the next round.

What You Need… and What To Do With It

Making a square

Make 6ch, sl st (slip stitch) into first ch to form a ring. Make 3ch, work 2dc (double crochet) into ring. *Make 3ch. Make 3dc (double crochet) into ring*. Repeat *to* twice more. Work 3 ch. Join with sl st into top of first 3ch to complete the square.

Joining in new yarn and changing colors

If the ball of yarn that you're using runs out or you want to introduce another color, you'll have to join in the new yarn.

If using single crochet, insert the hook as normal into the stitch using the original yarn and pull a loop through. Drop the old yarn and pick up the new yarn. Wrap new yarn over hook (1) and pull it through the two loops on the hook, in this way completing the double crochet. When using other stitches, join in same way, introducing new yarn on the last loop of the stitch. Try not to run out of yarn in the middle of a row. If you think you haven't got enough yarn to complete the next row, join in new yarn at the beginning of the row to create a neater piece of work that's easier to handle. Work ends of both old and new yarn over a couple of stitches and with scissors cut off the ends of both yarns to create a neat finish (2).

Increasing

Simple increasing means working a number of stitches into the same space. Increases can be made at the edges or at any point along a row or a round.

IN THE MIDDLE OF A ROW

Work one stitch as usual and then make another stitch in the same space as the previous stitch (1). Mark the position of the additional stitch with a contrasting color or a safety pin to show the placement of the increase for subsequent increases (2).

AT THE END OF A ROW

Work the turning chain as usual. For single crochet and half double crochet, work two stitches in the first stitch of the previous row. Continue along the row and increase where it is indicated in the pattern (3). For all taller stitches, remember that the turning chain counts as a first stitch, so for those stitches work on one extra stitch in the first stitch of the previous row. The edge will slant outwards.

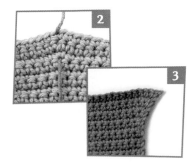

Decreasing

Decreasing is used to make the size of the work smaller. You can decrease in the middle of the work or at the edges. It is most frequently used at the edges to shape a piece of clothing at the underarm seams or around the neck.

AT THE BEGINNING OF A ROW

Add chains for a turning chain, skip a stitch, work a stitch in the next stitch and work across the row to the last two stitches.

AT THE END OF A ROW

Skip the next-to-last stitch and work a stitch in the last stitch.

IN THE MIDDLE OF A ROW

Skip a stitch and work the next stitch. Mark the beginning of the point of decrease with a contrasting color yarn or a safety pin to show where consequent increases should be.

DECREASING A DOUBLE CROCHET

Yoh, insert hook into top of next st, pull yarn through. Insert hook into top of next st, pull yarn through. Yoh, pull through 3sts, yoh, pull through last two sts (makes 1 decrease).

Fastening off/finishing

Although you only have one stitch to work on at once, you will need to fasten off so that your work doesn't unravel.

Cut your yarn leaving approximately a 6in (15cm) tail. Pull the tail through the loop on the hook and pull tightly (1).

Weaving/sewing in ends

Thread the yarn with a wool sewing needle or a blunt-ended needle with a large enough eye for the size of the yarn or thread.

Weave the needle in and out of stitches near the cast off edge and pull the yarn through (1). Cut off end neatly with a sharp pair of scissors.

  What You Need... and What To Do With It

★ How to read a crochet pattern

Reading a crochet pattern is something that puts many people off. The terminology can look very daunting and in this book I have tried to keep it as simple as possible and have included explanations in full where necessary.

Patterns are usually laid out in the same way, first showing the materials needed to make the item. Then giving you the brand name of the yarn with the shade numbers and the amount you'll need. If it is a garment there will be a different amount of yarn given for each size. A pattern will also give you the hook size you need and details of any other accessories. You will then be taken through a step-by-step, row-by-row instruction. Crochet uses abbreviations which will be listed with an explanation of what each one means.

The instructions are there to make the patterns make good, clear sense and should follow a logical pattern. For example "1sc in next st" means work one single crochet stitch in the next stitch in the row below. If you are an absolute beginner, it will become clear once you have worked through the "What You Need… And What To Do With It" section.

A pattern repeat can be given in several ways, the most usual is shown using an asterisk. For example: *3dc, 3ch, skip 3sts, rep from * to last 3sts. This means that you repeat the stitches instructed between the asterisks until you get to the end of the row, where you'll have 3sts left at the end and you'll be instructed to work according to the pattern. Another way to explain repeats is by putting the instruction into a bracket: (3dc, 3ch, skip 3sts) four times. This means repeat the instruction that is within the bracket four times.

If the pattern states "right side" or RS, make sure you mark it. A piece of crochet has no "right" or "wrong" side until it is given one, either because a stitch with a texture has been included or two pieces of yarn have been joined together leaving a tail on one side.

US and UK terminology differs considerably in crochet. It seems that in the US stitches are named after the number of loops on the hook *excluding* the first loop (see page 20) while in the UK it *includes* that loop. The chart below explains the differences in the descriptions of the stitches. The terminology used in this book is for the US.

DIFFERENCES IN COMMON CROCHET TERMINOLOGY

United States	United Kingdom
Slip stitch (sl st)	Slip stitch (ss)
Single crochet (sc)	Double crochet (dc)
Half double crochet (hdc)	Half treble (htr)
Double crochet (dc)	Treble (tr)
Treble (tr)	Double treble (dtr)
Double treble (dtr)	Triple treble (trtr)
Triple treble or Long treble (trtr)	Quadruple treble (quadtr)
Afghan stitch	Tunisian stitch
Skip	Miss
Gauge	Tension

★ Crochet beading

Thread the beads onto the yarn before you start to crochet. If the bead holes are too small to go through the eye of the needle use the following threading method.

Double thread a sewing needle (1). Loop the yarn through it and draw the bead over the tapestry needle over the thin cotton and onto the yarn (2). Always bead on a wrong-side row and place the bead to the back of the work.

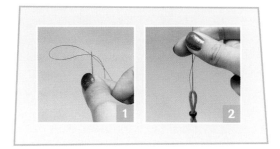

Beading on single crochet

Insert hook, wrap yarn over the hook (yoh), pull loop through, slide bead up yarn and place it close to the work (1). Yoh, (catch yarn beyond bead), pull through both loops on hook (2).

Beading on double crochets

Wrap yarn over the hook (yoh), insert hook, yoh and pull the two loops through. Slide a bead up the yarn and place it close to the work. Yoh (catch yarn beyond bead), and pull through both loops on hook. Continue with pattern instructions.

★ Seams

When joining crochet pieces make sure they are the correct size. Try and join motifs as they are being made and choose the type of seam that best suits the item and the yarn or thread. Use the same yarn or thread that is in the crochet, unless the yarn is particularly bulky or chunky. In this case you should use a finer matching yarn to prevent the seams from bunching up.

Back stitch seam

This is a hard-wearing seam, ideal for items such as bags and for areas of clothing where strength is an advantage, such as shoulder seams.

With the wrong side facing and the right sides together, match the stitches or rows. Using a wool sewing needle or needle with a big enough eye for the yarn or thread, sew in back stitch (1).

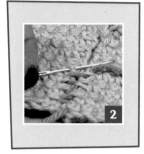

Woven seam

This is a flatter seam, suitable for finer pieces of crochet work.

Lay the pieces with the edges touching and the wrong side facing up. Then use a wool or tapestry sewing needle and weave around the centers of the edge stitches (2). Take care not to pull the stitches too tightly.

Slip stitch seam

This seam can be worked with the right sides together so the ridge of the seam is inside the work, or with the wrong sides together so that the ridge is shown on the right side of the work.

Put the hook into each corresponding stitch of each edge and work one slip stitch through each pair of stitches along the seam (3).

Single crochet seam

Sewing together crochet with single crochet is another simple way to join a seam. It can leave a ridge. This can either be used as a feature on the right side, or the seam can be single crocheted on the wrong side and then turned to reveal an invisible seam on the right side.

Insert the hook in each of the corresponding stitches along the seam and single crochet into each stitch until the end (4).

★ Edgings

Edgings are the perfect way to make a garment looked finished and professional. Knitted or crocheted garments can be livened up by a crocheted edging and they are easy to add on. Four easy edgings are explained below and opposite. Always start by making one row of single crochet to set the edging off. If using one color, continue as follows. If using a different color for the edging, join yarn by using a sl st.

Single crochet edging

Make 1ch. Insert the hook into each stitch along the row or round.

You will often need 3sc in each corner stitch otherwise the work will not lie flat.

Picot edging

Join yarn by using sl st.

ROW 1
1sc into each st, turn.

ROW 2
1sc *3ch, sl st into third ch from hook, skip 1st, 1sc into next st; rep from * to end.

Shell edging

Join yarn by using sl st.

ROW 1
1sc into each st, turn.

ROW 2
1sc *skip 1 st, 5dc into next st, skip 1st, 1sc into next st; rep from * to end.

Frill edging

The pattern for this stitch works in sections of eight stitches. So you need enough stitches so the total will divide equally by eight.

ROW 1

1sc into each st, turn.

ROW 2

*1ch, skip 1st, 1sc 1ch 1hdc in next st, skip 1st, 1dc 1ch 1dc in next st, skip 1st, 1hdc 1ch 1sc in next st, 1ch, skip 1st, 1sl st in next st, rep from * to end placing the last sl st in beginning of row. Turn 1ch.

ROW 3

*1sc, 1hdc in next ch sp, 3dc in next ch sp, 3tr 1ch 3tr in next ch sp, 3dc in next ch sp, 1hdc 1sc in next ch sp, 1sl st on sl st, rep from * to end. Fasten off.

Crochet through the decades

★ Embellishments

Pom-poms, tassels, flowers, fringes and crocheted buttons are all ways to make your crochet individual and unique. These easily made embellishments can make all the difference to a simple piece of fabric and turn it into something quite beautiful. Using the following instructions for different embellishments, try using up odd bits of yarn or balancing the main fabric with a differently textured yarn. In the pom-poms we added a few strands of lurex and a thick slub yarn, which gave them a rich texture.

What You Need... and What To Do With It

Pom-poms

Pom-poms can liven up a cushion, blanket, hat, scarf or dog coat. Try using strands of yarn in different colors to make multi-colored ones. When you have used up one color, just change to a different color.

Cut out two circles of cardboard (an empty cereal box will do nicely) to the size you want your pom-pom to be, using a cup or other circular utensil as a guide (1). Cut a small hole in the center of each circle (2). Place the two circles together. Wind some wool off a ball to make a small ball. Put the tail through the small circle and start winding it round the card and through the hole (3), until the hole is so small that you can't get any more wool through. For a thinner pom-pom, use less wool. When the last piece of yarn is used up, pull the yarn apart at the outer circle with both index fingers to reveal the card. Insert scissors between the two pieces of card. Holding the tail of yarn with your left hand, cut round the outer edge of the pom-pom (4). When you have cut all the way round, wind a separate piece of yarn between the two pieces of card. Secure very tightly in a double knot (5). Remove the two cards and trim the pom-pom.

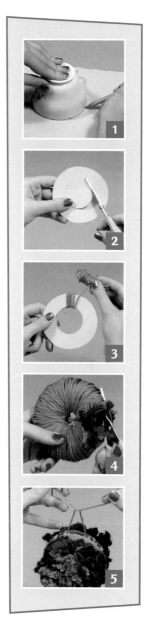

Mini pom-poms

If you want to make a mini pom-pom, the hole in the above method will be too small to push the yarn through. Here is a quick and easy method for making a mini pom-pom.

Wrap the yarn around two fingers 70 or 80 times. Slide the yarn bunch off your fingers and, holding on to one end of the bunch, pick up the yarn and wrap it around the center of the bunch tightly. Cut the yarn leaving a 10in (25cm) tail. Thread the yarn through a wool sewing needle and push the needle through the center where the yarn has been wrapped three or four times, then wrap the yarn around and push the needle through the center again so that it's wrapped very tightly. Break the yarn. Take some sharp scissors and cut through the loops at both ends. Fluff out the pom-pom and trim the ends to make an even sphere. To make the pom pom look very fluffy and dense, don't be afraid to cut it down quite severely.

Tassels

Find a cassette or CD case, or anything solid that is the required tassel length. Wrap wool round the object 30–40 times, depending on the thickness of the wool and how fat you want the tassel (1 and 2). Take another piece of yarn and thread it through the top of the wool on the object. Tie very tight with a double knot. Then pull all the wool off. Holding the top of the tassel with your left hand, cut the bottom to form tassels (3). Then cut a separate piece of yarn. Tie the yarn around the tassel and make a neck, wrapping the yarn around the tassel several times. Secure with a double knot (4). Thread the same piece of yarn with a sewing needle and push the needle from front to back several times to secure. Trim the bottom.

Fringes

Find a cassette or CD case, or anything solid that is the required length of the fringe. Wrap wool round the object four or five times, depending on the thickness of the wool and how fat you want the fringe (1). Slide the yarn off, holding it tightly at the top. Push the fringe up through the bottom loop of the item, using either your fingers or a crochet hook (2). Making a loop with the fringe, push the bottom of the tassel though it and pull tight (3). Trim the bottom strands.

What You Need… and What To Do With It

Little flower

Make 6ch, sl st into first ch to form a ring.

ROUND 1
1ch, work 15sc into ring, sl st into first sc.

ROUND 2
3ch, dc2tog as follows over next 2sc. Yoh, insert hook into next st, yoh and pull through. Yoh, pull through two loops (leaving two loops on hook). Yoh, insert hook into next st and pull through. Yoh, pull through two loops, yoh and pull through all three loops. Sl st into next sc. Repeat from *to* four times, making five petals, placing last sl st into last sc of previous round. Fasten off.

Pierrot button

Make 3ch, make a ring with 1sl st.

ROUND 1
3ch, 12dc into center of ring, join with 1sl st to top of 3ch.

ROUND 2
1ch, 1sc in each dc, 1sl st to join.

ROUND 3
As Round 2.
Leave a long end, approx 8in (20cm). Using a tapestry needle, weave the end through the stitches. Cut some of the same yarn off the ball and fill the center of the button very firmly. Using the loose end of the yarn, draw the stitches tightly together. Fasten off and use the same thread to attach the button to your item.

Two-color button

Make 3ch, form a ring with 1sl st.

ROUND 1
1ch, 5sc into ring with first color. Fasten off.

ROUND 2
Using second color, 3ch, 1dc in same st, 2dc into each sc to end. Join with 1sl st. Thread a 8in (20cm) yarn end through each st and finish by filling the center of the button firmly with yarn from same ball. Using the loose end of the yarn, draw the stitches tightly together. Fasten off.

★ Where to buy yarn and cottons

If you are under the impression that the only yarn available is the itchy woolen stuff, or the acrylic type that makes your hair stand on end, then think again. The new yarns that have taken over are soft, fleecy, sometimes wacky, and in textures and colors beyond your wildest yarn dreams.

Wool is no longer something you have to buy to make cheap clothes for your family; it can now be regarded as an exotic textile, a piece of art, something to satisfy your senses. It's worth searching around for yarns just to discover the textures and the new sumptuous colors available.

INTERNET YARN SUPPLIERS

Probably the best places to source your yarn are Internet yarn suppliers, and more and more people are now following this trend and shopping online. These suppliers often have a much wider range to offer than traditional shops and will mail directly to your door. Make sure you find an Internet company that has a good range of photographs of the yarn and the patterns available, and offers you the option to returns any yarn that doesn't live up to expectations. It can be a real pleasure shopping for wool online, especially when you receive your parcel full of crochet goodies–it's just like having a present delivered through the mail.

DEPARTMENT STORES

Supplies can be limited through department stores, but with the new popularity in crafts in general, stores are beginning to expand their yarn ranges.

WOOL STORES

The small wool and haberdashery stores of old have mostly closed down. There is, however, a new wave of wool stores that are emerging: they're spacious, open-plan, and sometimes have an area for cappuccinos. Often they offer workshops in crochet and knitting.

CHARITY STORES

The tradition of unravelling a garment and reusing the wool to make something new still has a valid place, so if you're trying to crochet on a tight budget, go along to your local charity store where you can nearly always find something hand-knitted or crocheted. It's also a good place to unearth yarns and cottons that people have never used, those that have been hoarded in attics for years.

Wherever possible, try to use the brand and type of yarn specified in the pattern. However, yarns can also be substituted, in which case you should match the weight and length of the substitute yarn. Also check the hook size that is recommended in the pattern as this can give you a general guide to the yarn thickness and enable you to find a substitute. Always make a gauge square (see page 18) and adjust your needle size accordingly.

What You Need... and What To Do With It

★ Carrying and storing yarn and crochet

A PORTABLE CRAFT

Crochet is one of the most portable crafts. Unlike knitting, which requires two pointed needles, crochet has only one small hook that can easily pop inside a neat little bag, ready to be whipped out and used at the earliest opportunity. There is also only one stitch, so if it slips off the hook for any reason you only have one stitch to pick up.

Crochet is often worked in small patchwork squares and then sewn together, so projects are usually easy to carry around.

STORING YARN

The luscious colors and sumptuous feel of merino, alpaca, cashmere, angora, and fancy yarns look so appealing that people buy them solely as a stylish interior feature that can be displayed proudly in a basket within a room. The colors that are popular in yarn now tend to match designer paint palettes and no longer have to be hidden in the attic to waste away.

However, if you decide you have so much spare yarn that you need to put some away safely, make sure the yarn is stored in a dry area. Plastic boxes with lids are useful, or alternatively put the yarn in a plastic bag inside a basket or box. The last thing you want is mice getting ahold of your precious fiber, or the cat infesting it with fleas.

STORING HOOKS

Hooks are small things and, like ballpoint pens, tend to get lost. Find an attractive pot to keep them in for easy access.

★ Washing, blocking and steaming

Washing

Creating your own piece of crochet takes considerable time and trouble and the last thing you want is to ruin your work by washing it incorrectly.

Yarn labels usually have international labelling standards for their care. Most yarns can be successfully cleaned by careful hand washing. Check the label and if the yarn can be machine washed make sure you set the machine to the recommended temperature.

General hand-washing instructions

✴ Use detergent that is recommended for hand washing and dissolve it in the water before immersing your garment. Make sure the water is only hand hot.

✴ Rinse the garment twice in cooler water.

✴ Give the garment a short spin in the machine, or if the item is very delicate place it in a towel and gently squeeze out the excess moisture.

✴ Work the garment carefully into shape and place on a dry towel on a flat surface, or on a clothes line to dry.

Machine washing

The label should give the recommended temperature at which to set the machine. General temperature guidelines:

140°F–too hot to the touch
120°F–hand hot
104°F–warm to the touch
86°F–cool

Washing special yarns

✴ Lightweight and mercerized cottons are best washed by hand.

✴ Heavyweight cottons are fine to wash in the machine on a cool wash, and should then be dried flat.

✴ Fancy yarns, such as lurex, mohair and chenille, can be dry cleaned–check the labels.

✴ Leather, string, raffia and sisal constructions should be wiped down with a cloth or sponge and left to dry.

Ironing

Ironing your crocheted fabric can make the difference between it looking like a professional piece of art or an old rag.

Yarn with a high content of natural fiber can be ironed, but some yarn can be totally ruined by a hot iron. Check the label for the ironing instructions–it should give you all the help you need, other than switching the iron on for you! Yarn labels are very useful for telling you at which temperature to set the iron, or whether you need a damp or a dry cloth.

1990s

Crochet through the decades

Damp finishing

If you are instructed that the yarn is not to be ironed, then follow the instructions below:

First of all find a colorfast towel and then make it damp. The next stage is to lie the towel flat, lay your pieces of fabric on the towel and roll them up together loosely. Leave like this for approximately one hour so that the crocheted piece absorbs the dampness from the towel.

Undo the towel on a flat surface and place the pieces once more on top of it. Pin the pieces into shape with pins (blocking). Find another damp cloth or towel and lay it over the top so your fabric is sandwiched. Press gently down onto your fabric so every part of it is touching the cloth and leave it to dry in a place that is not going to stay damp for too long, or it will smell musty–a laundry room is ideal.

Blocking

This is a method used to keep your garment in shape while it is drying. It is also used as a method to pin a garment out into shape before sewing it up, especially for any pieces that tend to curl up at the edges.

After washing and when the fabric has had the moisture squeezed out and is still damp, shape it into position on a dry towel ideally placed on a padded surface. Ease the fabric into place, right side facing upwards, to achieve the correct measurements. Then pin out the pieces using large-headed colored pins (this is where the padding comes into its own). Make a point of placing the pins on the very outer edges of the fabric.

PART THREE

Cool Girl's Patterns…

… To Get You Hooked

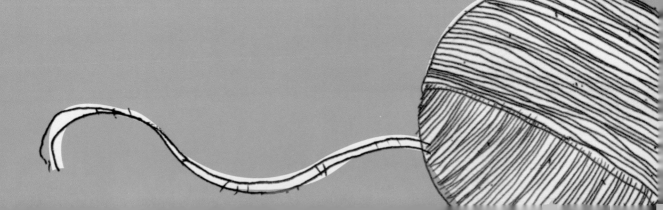

The yarn starts here…

Crochet trends have changed dramatically in recent years and in the 20 patterns that follow the yarns, designs and crochet pieces have been chosen to represent the new and stylish ways of using this absorbing and versatile craft. Crochet was traditionally associated with fine threads and intricate work using hooks often little bigger than a tapestry needle. But in the late 20th century the abundance of thicker, natural and creatively mixed yarns in the marketplace hailed an upsurge in the popularity of crochet. The craft is all around us–just look in the fashion pages of consumer magazines and supplements, as well as on the fashion catwalks, to find crocheted inspiration. Every one of our patterns is designed to be as simple as possible so that beginners will feel comfortable and unthreatened by any complicated stitches, but the items are all so tempting that even the seasoned, or lapsed, crocheter will be lured towards picking up the hook again.

When deciding what to crochet, many people want to make something special for their home, so with this in mind there are two beautiful patterns for cushions; one round (see the cushion cake on page 84) and one square (see the loopy cushion on page 87). They both have an individuality that can be adapted by changing the color scheme to suit any décor. The cushions use Rooster Aran yarns, which comes in a mix of alpaca and pure wool and are perfect for snuggling up to at the end of the sofa. The flower blanket on page 48 is made up of simple squares and is soft, luxurious and made in beautiful colors. The squares make it a perfect ongoing project as you can work on one or two squares in an evening and then put your work down until you feel like starting again. As opposed to knitting, where the dropped stitches on half-finished work can drive the knitter to distraction, crochet only ever has one loop on the hook at a time so you don't lose your stitches when you put it down. And then when you go to bed, why not curl up with the warm and toasty hot-water bottle cover with pom-pom ties (see page 82). Made using Rowan Big wool, a thick superchunky wool that is quick and easy to work with, this can be made in one evening–especially when the temperature plummets!

Bolero and wrap-over cardigans are elegant and fashionable and we've combined both into one garment–the tie bolero cardigan on page 63 can be tied at the front, or wrapped around and tied at the back or on the side. It uses Debbie Bliss Baby Cashmerino yarn, a soft, light yarn that shows the stitch detail without being bulky. The same yarn is used to make the daisy cashmere scarf on page 73, made with simple squares decorated with little pom-poms instead of the traditional fringe. This scarf can also be combined with the elegant fingerless gloves with lace edgings shown on page 76. Made using Debbie Bliss Alpaca Silk, these feel so glorious to wear that you won't ever want to take them off!

It seems that many people nowadays also want to create their own fashion accessories, so we've included some fantastic items that complement any cool outfit. They are also perfect gifts; a homemade gift is so much nicer and more satisfying than store-bought gifts. Once made, and presented wrapped in colored tissue and tied with a ribbon this looks as good as anything you can buy commercially.

Ribbon and flowers have been used in many of the patterns: a simple crochet flower or a piece of ribbon enables the transformation of a plain-looking garment or accessory into something quite individual. The flower-power beaded belt on page 68 combines beads, flowers and ribbon, providing the perfect accessory for a light summer skirt and just as effective threaded through the belt loops of a denim skirt or jeans.

The beanie hats on page 46 went down so well that we made loads of them in different colors. This simple design uses basic stitches and is a good introduction to shaping techniques. Our other hat is a very pretty summer brimmed hat (see page 70), an ideal strategy for keeping the sun off with style. The ribbon slippers on page 80 are quite divine–they are so cute and come in three different sizes and you may find that your friends and family will be begging you to make some for them. The glamorous frill shawl on page 50 is made using a fine mohair yarn called Rowan Kid Silk Haze, which comes in an impressive range of elegant colors. The popular teal shade is shown as the main color, edged with the addition of a frill in rose pink that sways and swishes and makes the wearer feel like Marilyn Monroe.

There are two crochet bag patterns. One of them is a delicate beaded purse (see page 78), which is a very pretty accessory for a little evening number when just a minimum of items needs to be carried. The mesh bag (see page 60) is bright, colorful and funky, made using Colinette Point Five chunky yarn and a double knit cotton. This bag makes a definite fashion statement and is for girls who want to make a strong impression.

Finally we come to our pets–and how could we possibly forget about them! Marley, our model puppy, couldn't believe his luck when we designed and made a stripey dog blanket especially for him (see page 56). The stripes hide the dog hairs and muddy paws and the blanket is made using the fabulous Rooster Aran yarn. We used each of the Rooster Aran range of colors which make a perfect matching color palette. The blanket can be made in two sizes–large and small– depending on the size of your puppy. This blanket has the added flexibility that you can use any type of yarn and work it to any size, as it has no shaping–and it's made using a simple half double crochet stitch. If I were less of a pet lover I would say it was too good to be a pet blanket. We have equally spoiled Pebbles the cat, a rather funky cat that well suits the pet's playmat on page 52. The cosy mat is made in the round so Pebbles doesn't have to look round corners for his prey, and has a swishy tasselled edge that he can play with when the mice are sleeping.

The designers involved with creating the patterns included here are principally young design experts working in the textile industry with fresh new ideas to bring to the newly revived craft of crochet. The final range of uplifting patterns that we have selected for this book is testimony to the endurance of a craft that has proved itself able to switch and change according to current trends. Crochet has once again emerged from its hidden cocoon to demonstrate its adaptability and its beauty–a craft that now represents the essence of cool.

2000s

Crochet through the decades

Abbreviations

ch	chain	alt	alternate
sl st	slip stitch	approx	approximately
dc	double crochet	beg	beginning
htr	half treble	ch sp	chain space
tr	treble	cc	contrasting color
dtr	double treble	cont	continue
trtr	triple treble	dec	decrease
qtr	quadruple treble	foll	following
		in	inch(es)
		inc	increase
		lp(s)	loop(s)
		m	meter(s)
		MC	main colour
		mm	millimeter(s)
		patt(s)	pattern(s)
		rem	remain
		rep	repeat
		RS	right side
		sp(s)	space(s)
		st(s)	stitch(es)
		t-ch	turning chain
		tog	together
		WS	wrong side
		yoh	yarn over hook

Beanie hat

This simple beanie hat, made in one size, uses three basic stitches and is an ideal first project. It looks great in any color, or if you feel ambitious try creating stripes (see page 25 for joining in new yarn). Add a flower or a pom-pom, or change to a textured wool to alter the look completely.

MATERIALS

Rooster Almerino Aran (50g balls)
shade 307, Brighton Rock x 2 balls

Crochet hook: size G/6

STITCHES USED

single crochet, slip stitch, half double crochet, double crochet

ABBREVIATIONS

ch chain	sc single crochet
dec decrease	hdc half double crochet
sl st slip stitch	dc double crochet

METHOD

All sts are worked into back loop of sc, hdc, dc.

Round 1: Make 90ch, sl st into first ch.

Round 2: 1ch (counts as first sc) 1sc into each ch to end. Sl st into top of first sc.

Rounds 3–6: Repeat Round 2, four more times.

Round 7: 2ch (counts as 1st hdc) 1hdc into each sc until end of round. Sl st into top of first hdc.

Rounds 8–11: Repeat Round 7, four more times.

Round 12: 3ch 1dc into each hdc, sl st into top of first dc.

Round 13: 3ch (counts as first dc) 6dc, dec 1st (yoh, insert hook into top of next st, pull yarn through, insert hook into top of next st, pull yarn through, yoh, pull through first 3sts, yoh, pull through last 2sts) *7dc, dec 1st*. Repeat from * to * to end. Sl st into top of first 3ch.

Round 14: 3ch (counts as 1st dc) 5dc, dec 1st *6dc, dec 1st*. Repeat from * to * to end. Sl st into top of first 3ch.

Round 15: 2ch (counts as first hdc) 4hdc, dec 1st (same as before) *5hdc, dec 1st*. Repeat from * to * to end. Sl st into top of first 2ch.

Round 16: 2ch (counts as first hdc) 3hdc, dec 1st *4hdc, dec 1st*. Repeat from * to * to end. Sl st into top of first 2ch.

Round 17: 2ch (counts as first hdc) 2hdc, dec 1st *3hdc, dec 1st*. Repeat from * to * to end. Sl st into top of first 2ch.

Round 18: 3ch (counts as first dc) 1dc, dec 1st *2dc, dec 1st*. Repeat from * to * to end. Sl st into top of first 3ch.

Round 19: 3ch (counts as first dc) dec 1st *1dc, dec 1st*. Repeat from * to * to end. Sl st into top of first 3ch.

Round 20: 3ch (counts as first dc) 1dc into each dc to end. Sl st into top of first 3ch.

Finishing

With wool sewing needle and 8in (20cm) yarn, weave in and of top of the last row of double crochet around top of hat. Hold beginning of yarn and pull together until the hole is closed. Fasten off by making a knot and sew yarn ends in neatly.

Cool Girl's Patterns... To Get You Hooked

Flower blanket

The mixture of colors in this blanket complement each other beautifully. The squares are very straightforward; as soon as you've got the hang of one, you just have to do another 59. The blanket is a real showpiece in any home.

MEASUREMENTS

Each square measures 6½ x 6½in (16.5 x 16.5cm)
Overall size of throw approximately 39 x 65in (99 x 165cm)

MATERIALS

Rooster Almerino Aran (50g balls)
Yarn A: shade 301, Cornish x 5 balls
Yarn B: shade 302, Sugared Almond x 1 ball
Yarn C: shade 306, Gooseberry x 5 balls
Yarn D: shade 304, Mushroom x 11 balls
Yarn E: shade 303, Strawberry Cream x 1 ball
Yarn F: shade 307, Brighton Rock x 1 ball
Yarn G: shade 305, Custard x 1 ball

Crochet hook: size J/10

STITCHES USED

chain, single crochet, treble, slip stitch, double crochet

ABBREVIATIONS

ch chain	ch sp chain space
sc single crochet	tr treble
sl st slip stitch	dc double crochet
WS wrong side	

METHOD

All stitches to be worked into back of each st.

Round 1: Using yarn A make 4ch, join with a sl st.

Round 2: Into center of ring make 3sc, 2ch *3sc, 2ch*. Repeat from * to * twice more and join with a sl st into top of first sc. Break yarn.

Round 3: Join in color B, E, F or G (work 15 squares alternating these colors).
Make 6ch *3tr, 2ch, 3tr, 2ch into next ch sp (corner)*. Repeat into next two corners. Work 3tr, 2ch, 2tr into next corner ch sp, sl st into fourth of first 6ch. Break yarn.

Round 4: Join new yarn by putting hook through next ch sp, pull new color through and sl st. 3ch, 2dc into same ch sp, *2ch 3dc 3ch 3dc into next corner (next ch sp). 2ch, 3dc into next ch sp* Repeat from * to * twice more.
2ch, 3dc, 3ch, 3dc into next corner (ch sp).
2ch, sl st into top of first 3ch.
Break yarn.

Round 5: Join in yarn A. Make 1ch. Work 1sc into top edge of all stitches of previous row, at each corner work 1sc 1ch 1sc into center ch. Join with a sl st. Break yarn.

Round 6: Join in yarn D. Make 1ch. Work 1sc into top edge of all stitches from previous row, at each corner work 1sc 1ch 1sc into center chain. Join with sl st into first chain.

Round 7: Repeat Round 6.
Break yarn.

Make 15 squares of each petal color.

Finishing

Take two squares and hold WS together. Using yarn D join squares with a single crochet seam (see page 29).
Join work in strips vertically and then horizontally.

Edging

Using yarn D, sc in each stitch all the way round; in each corner make 2sc into corner stitch.
Sew in yarn ends neatly.

Frill shawl

This truly elegant garment made with Rowan Kid Silk Haze is light and soft and available in a range of beautiful colors. An excellent beginner's project, this shawl consists mainly of a series of chain stitches. It's made in one size and is crocheted using diamond net stitch edged with a line of single crochet, topped off with a frill edging. Remember to keep your gauge fairly loose otherwise it will be tricky picking up the chains when forming the diamond net stitch.

MEASUREMENTS
Approximately 67 x 27½in (170 x 70cm)

MATERIALS
Rowan Kid Silk Haze (25g balls)
Yarn A (main color): shade 582, Trance x 2 balls
Yarn B (edging): shade 583, Blushes x 2 balls

Crochet hook: size E/4

STITCHES USED
chain, single crochet, slip stitch, treble

ABBREVIATIONS
ch chain	ch sp chain space
sc single crochet	sl st slip stitch
tr treble	

METHOD
Make a foundation chain of 140ch, plus 2ch to turn (the number of chains must be a multiple of 4+2ch).

Row 1: Make 1sc in second chain from hook. *make 5ch, skip 3ch, 1sl st in next ch* Repeat from * to * to end. Make 7ch, turn.
Row 2: *Make 1sl st in third ch in center of first 5ch arch, 5ch* repeat from * to * across row ending with 1sl st in third ch of last arch, 2ch, work 1tr in last stitch, 6ch, turn.
Row 3: 1sl st in third ch of first 5ch arch. *5ch, 1sl st in third ch of next arch* repeat from * to * across 7ch, turn.

Repeat Rows 2 and 3 for the rest of the pattern until you have crocheted 140 rows.

Frill edging
To achieve a neat, professional finish it is always a good idea to start with one row of single crochet to set the edging off. Continue using yarn A to start your edging as follows:

Using yarn A, work 1sc into each stitch across width until corner. Work 3sc into corner stitch. Continuing along length, *make 3sc into each ch sp, 1sc into top of next st*. Repeat from *to* until corner. Work 3sc into corner st. Work each width and each length once more. Sl st to join. Fasten off.

Sew in yarn ends.

Tip: At this point hold the floating end of yarn parallel with the fabric edge and work your sc over it. This ensures easy finishing, allowing you to confidently snip off the ends knowing that your work will not unravel.

At the beginning of one of the long sides, join using yarn B. Work *20ch, sl st into next stitch, work 10ch sl st into next stitch* repeat from * to * until you have completely worked the edging all round the piece. Fasten off neatly.

Pet's playmat

This charming round mat is perfect for your pampered pussy cat to frolic on, so he can squeeze in those much-needed hours of napping without dragging himself to the sofa! It is crocheted in a round on a slightly smaller hook than usual to give a firm fabric in which claws are less liable to catch. You can invent color combinations to suit your cat's personality and your décor, choosing from the luscious Rooster color palette. When you start you may think the mat is "frilling", but by the end of Round 6 it should begin to lie flat, and then gets flatter the further out you work.

MATERIALS

Rooster Almerino Aran (50g balls)

Yarn A (main color): shade 308, Spiced Plum x 2 balls

Yarn B: shade 310, Rooster x 2 balls

Yarn C: shade 307, Brighton Rock x 2 balls

Yarn D: shade 305, Custard x 3 balls

Crochet hook: size G/6

STITCHES USED

single crochet, double crochet, treble crochet, slip stitch

ABBREVIATIONS

ch chain

dc double crochet

sl st slip stitch

sc single crochet

tr treble

METHOD

Using yarn A make 6ch. Join with a sl st in first ch to form a ring.

Round 1: 2ch, make 12sc into middle of circle, sl st into second of first 2ch. Do not turn at the end of this round or any throughout the pattern. (12sts)

Round 2: 2ch, make 3sc into next st (make 3sc into next st). Repeat all round the circle, sl st into second of first 2ch. (36sts)

Round 3: 2ch, make 3sc into next st, 1sc into each of next 2sts (3sc into next st, 1sc into each of next 2sts). Repeat all round circle. Sl st into second of first 2ch. (60sts)

Round 4: (make 5ch, 1sc into fourth st). Repeat all round circle. Sl st into first ch (this leaves 15 loops around the outside of circle).

Round 5: 2ch (5sc into space of loop) repeat all round the circle, sl st in second of first 2ch. (75sts)

Round 6: 3ch, starting in the next st make 1dc into each of next 9sts, 2dc into next st. (1dc into each of next 8sts, 2dc into next st, 1dc into each of next 9sts. 2dc into next st). Repeat all round circle. 1sl st into first 3ch. (84sts)

Round 7: This is where the circle begins to grow evenly and methodically; what you are actually doing is increasing 12sts throughout the round. If you find that the increases are causing the circle to have points, then stagger the increases periodically. 4ch, starting in the next st (these 4ch at the beginning of rounds count as the first tr). (1tr into each of next 6sts, 2tr into next st). Repeat all round circle, 1sl st into fourth of first 4ch. (96sts)

Round 8: 4ch, starting in the next st (1tr into each of next 7sts,

2tr into next st). Repeat all round circle. Sl st into fourth of first 4ch. (108sts)

Round 9: 4ch, starting in the next st (1tr into each of next 8sts, 2tr into next st). Repeat all round circle. Sl st into fourth of first 4ch. (120sts)

Rounds 10 and 11: Repeat Round 9 twice, making one more tr between each increase, as is shown in Round 7 (132sts), Round 8 (148sts), and Round 9. (156sts)

Round 12: Using yarn B, starting in the next st, (1tr into each of next 11sts, 2tr into next st). Repeat all round circle. Sl st into fourth of first 4ch. (168sts)

Rounds 13, 14, 15, 16: Repeat Round 12 four more times, making one more tr between each increase as is shown in Rounds 7, 8 and 9. (226sts)

Rounds 17: Using yarn C, 4ch, starting in the next st (1tr in each of the next 16sts, 2tr into next st). Repeat all round circle. Sl st into fourth of first 4ch. (238sts)

Rounds 18, 19, 20: Repeat Round 17 three more times, making one more tr between each increase as is shown in Rounds 7, 8 and 9. (274sts)

Round 21: Using yarn D, 4ch, starting in the next st (1tr into each of next 20sts, 2tr in the next st). Repeat all round circle. Sl st into fourth of first 4ch. (268sts)

Round 22: Repeat Round 21 once, making one more tr between each increase as is shown in Rounds 7, 8 and 9. (298sts). Fasten off.

Finishing
Neatly sew in ends.
Block gently, shaping into a circle as you work.

To make the fringe
1. Cut a piece of card that is 4¾ x 8in (12 x 20cm).
2. Using yarn D, wrap the yarn completely around the narrower width of the card five times, finishing at the same edge as you started.
3. Cut the yarn along the long edge of the card.
4. Keeping the yarn folded, slip it off the card and with your crochet hook pull the loop of folded yarn through a chain space on the outside of the circle.
5. Catch the long ends of the yarn into the hook and pull them through the loop you have just made.
6. Tug the ends to make a tight knot onto the edge.
7. Repeat this in every other chain around the circle.
8. When fringe is finished, trim and tidy any stray threads around the edge.

Summer flower camisole

This beautiful and feminine camisole goes well with either jeans or an elegant skirt.

MEASUREMENTS
To fit bust 32/34/36in (82/87/92cms)
Actual size 33/35/37in (84/89/94cms)

MATERIALS
(50g balls)
Rowan 4 ply cotton shade 131, Fresh x 5 balls
Rowan Cotton Glacé in the following shades: 811 Tickle;
815 Excite; 747 Candy Floss; 814 Shoot x 1 ball each

Crochet hook: size B/1

 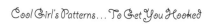

GAUGE

16sts and 9 rows of pattern to 2in (5cm) on size B/1 crochet hook using half double crochet.

STITCHES USED

half double crochet, single crochet, double crochet

ABBREVIATIONS

ch chain
hdc half double crochet
nxt next
RS right side
rep repeat

ch sp chain space
sl st slip stitch
tch turning chain
WS wrong side
tr double crochet

METHOD

Body (for both front and back)

Using the B/1 hook, make a chain of 135/143/151. This includes two extra chains for base row.

Work 1hdc into fifth chain from hook, 1ch *skip 1ch, 1hdc, 1ch rep* to last 2ch, 1hdc into last ch of base row. 66/70/74 spaces.

Row 1 (WS): 2ch, work 1hdc, 1ch into each 1ch sp until last 1ch sp, work 1hdc into space, 1hdc into second ch of tch, turn.

Row 2: 3ch, skip first 2hdc, 1hdc into nxt 1ch sp, *1ch, 1hdc into each 1ch sp rep* to tch, 1ch 1hdc into second ch of tch, turn. Repeat the last two rows until work measures 15½/16/16½in (39/40.5/42cm).

End with a WS row.

Front top shaping

With RS facing, work 3ch, skip first 2hdc *1hdc, 1ch into nxt space*, 31/33/35 times, turn.

Nxt, skip first ch sp, work 1hdc, 1ch 25/27/29 times, turn, skip first ch sp, work 1hdc, 1ch 23/25/27 times, turn.

Skip first ch sp, work 1hdc, 1ch 21/23/35 times, turn.

*Skip first ch sp, work 1hdc, 1ch 19/21/23 times, turn.

Skip first ch sp, work 1hdc, 1ch 17/19/21 times, turn*.

Continue to work as set, working 1hdc, 1ch, decreasing the number of times the repeats are worked by two on each row until all sizes have worked: skip first ch sp, work 1hdc, 1ch five times.

Total of 12/13/14 rows worked.

Working on these remaining sts, work as main patt, rep until it measures 9/9½/10in (23/24/25cm) from end of top shaping (this forms the strap). Turn work around and working with WS facing repeat the shaping for the other side.

Back top shaping

Work same as front shaping, but end after second row of strap.

Sewing up

Join side seams, starting 2in (5cm) from bottom edge.

Join straps by placing both front and back straps (with both RS facing outwards), join together with a flat seam.

Flowers

(make five of each different color)

Using a B/1 hook, make 8ch and join with a sl st to form a ring.

Round 1: Work 2ch, 1hdc into ring 14 times, join with a sl st in first 2ch.

Round 2: Work 6ch, *skip 2hdc, sl st into nxt hdc, 6ch, rep* to end, sl st into first ch of row. Five loops made.

Round 3: Into first loop on ring, work 1sc, 2hdc, 2dc, 2hdc, 1sc, work the same into each loop, sl st into first sc. Fasten off.

Finishing

Sew on the flowers to the top using the ends of each one. Place one flower of any color over the back join of the strap, then place the rest of the flowers however you wish. Embroider the stems connecting the flowers using a running stitch.

Stripy dog blanket

This is the height of luxury for your favorite pooch. The blanket is striped in a durable half double crochet stitch, so it's tough and the multi-colored stripes hide the dirt or hairs. The colors blend so it suits any shade of dog fur, but play around with the colors to get the perfect combination. Crochet the size of the blanket to the size of your dog. You can also use any yarn, so if you have lots of scraps and ends, it's a great way to use them all up. You may end up loving it so much that you keep the blanket for yourself!

MEASUREMENTS
Small: 37½ x 29½in (95 x 75cm)
Large: 53in x 107in (134 x 107cm)

MATERIALS
Rooster Almerino Aran (50g balls)
shade 301, Cornish; shade 302, Sugared Almond; shade 303, Strawberry Cream; shade 304, Mushroom; shade 305, Custard; shade 306, Gooseberry; shade 307, Brighton Rock; shade 308, Spiced Plum; shade 309, Ocean; shade 310, Rooster
x 1 ball of each shade (small size)
x 2 balls of each shade (large size)

Crochet hook: size H/8

STITCHES USED
half double crochet

ABBREVIATIONS
ch chain   hdc half double crochet
st stitch

METHOD
Change yarn color on each row.

Make 114 (166)ch, turn.

Each row: 2ch (counts as first hdc) work 1hdc into each st to end, turn. Repeat.

Continue until work measures 29.5in (75cm) (small), 42in (107cm) (large). Fasten off.

Finishing
Sew in yarn ends.

Striped hairbands

These hairbands are refreshingly quick, inexpensive and easy to make. They make ideal gifts and can be crocheted in a single evening. They're also an excellent beginner's project as well as good for learning how to join colors.

MATERIALS
Rowan Handknit Cotton (50g balls)
Yarn A: shade 219, Gooseberry x 1 ball
Yarn B: shade 253, Tope x 1 ball
Yarn C: shade 315, Double Choc x 1 ball
Yarn D: shade 254, Flame x 1 ball

Crochet hook: size F/5

STITCHES USED
chain stitch, single crochet, slip stitch

ABBREVIATIONS
ch chain stitch	sc single crochet
sl st slip stitch	st stitch

METHOD
Row 1: Using yarn A make 75ch, turn work.

Row 2: Make 1ch, skip first st of previous row, 1sc into each stitch along row, turn work.

Row 3: Change to yarn B. Make 1ch, skip first st of previous row, 1sc into each stitch along row, turn work. Break yarn.

Row 4: Change to yarn C, make 1ch, skip first st off previous row, 1sc into each stitch along row, fasten off last stitch.

Row 5: Using yarn D, make 25ch, join yarn onto last st of previous row. 1sc into each st along row, make 25ch. Fasten off (this row forms the ties).

Row 6: Using color C join yarn back to last sc of previous row, 1sc into each sc st of previous row, turn work. Break yarn.

Row 7: Using color B, make 1ch, skip first st of previous row, 1sc into each stitch along row, turn work. Break yarn.

Row 8: Using color A, make 1ch, skip first st, 1sc into each stitch along row, turn work.

Row 9: 1 sl st into each st along row, fasten off.

Finishing
Sew in yarn ends.

Mesh bag

This bag is stylish enough to carry around even if it's empty. It is made up of two side pieces, a base and strap in Debbie Bliss cotton and the front and back panels in Colinette Point Five Yarn. The handle is made of rope covered in Debbie Bliss Cotton. Buttons are used to decorate the front and back mesh panels. The bag is great for all seasons; it can either be used as a beach bag or as a winter accessory.

MATERIALS
(50g balls)
Yarn A: Debbie Bliss Cotton DK, shade 15, Red x 4 balls
(100g hanks)
Yarn B: Colinette Point Five, shade Jamboree x 2 hanks
59in (150cm) rope/washing line
28 black shiny shirt buttons, ½in (1cm) diameter

Crochet hooks: size D/3 and size F/5

STITCHES USED
single crochet, double crochet, chain, slip stitch

ABBREVIATIONS

ch chain	sc single crochet
ch sp chain space	dc double crochet
sp space	sl st slip stitch
rem remaining	t-ch turning chain
rep repeat	st(s) stitch(es)
alt alternately	

METHOD

Bag base
Use yarn A and crochet hook size D/3
Make 52ch.
Row 1: 1sc into second ch from hook, 1sc into each rem ch, 1t-ch.
Row 2: Skip first sc, 1sc into each rem sc, 1t-ch.
Rows 3–17: Rep Row 2 15 times.
Row 18: Skip first sc, 1sc into each rem sc to end of row, one extra sc into last sc. Turn to short side of piece and 1sc into each row, one extra sc into end row, turn to long side (base of piece), 1sc into base of each sc, one extra sc into end sc, 1sc into each row, one extra sc into end row. Fasten off.

Side panels
Use yarn A, crochet hook D/3. Make 20ch.
Row 1: 1sc into third ch from hook, 1sc into each rem ch, 3t-ch.
Row 2: Skip first sc, 2dc into next 2sc, (2ch, skip 2sc, 3dc into next 3sc) to end of row, 3t-ch.
Rows 3–18: Rep Row 2 16 times.
Row 19: Skip 2sc, 1dc. (2ch, skip 2sc, 3dc into next 3sc) twice. 2ch, skip 2ch, 1dc, skip 1dc, 3t-ch.
Row 20: 2ch, (skip 2ch and 1dc), 3dc into next 3sts, 2ch, skip 2ch, 3dc into next 3sts, 2ch, (skip 2ch and 1dc), 1dc, 3t-ch.
Row 21: Skip 2ch, 3dc into next 3sts, 2ch, skip 2ch, 4dc into next 4sts, 3t-ch.
Row 22: Skip first dc, 3dc into next 3sts, 2ch, skip 2ch, 4dc into next 4sts, 3t-ch.
Rows 23–29: Rep Row 22 seven times.
Row 30: Skip first st, 1sc into each st to end. Fasten off.

Front and back panels
Use yarn B and crochet hook H/8. Make 37ch.
Row 1: 1sc into third ch from hook, 1sc into each rem ch to end, 3t-ch.
Row 2: Skip first sc, (3dc into next 3sc, 2ch, skip 2sc) five times, 2ch, skip 2sc, 4dc into next 4sc, 3t-ch.
Rows 3–4: Rep Row 2 twice.
Row 5: Skip first dc, 3dc into next 3sts, 1sc, (ch7, skip 4sts, 1sc into fifth st) five times. Skip 1ch, 4dc into next 4sts, 3t-ch.
Row 6: Skip first dc, 1dc, 1sc, (6ch, 1sc into top of loop) five times. ch6, (skip 3ch and 1dc) 1sc into second dc, 2dc into next 2sts, 3t-ch.
Row 7: Skip 2sts, 4dc into next 4sts, 1sc. (7ch, 1sc into top of loop) four times. 7ch, 1sc into top of loop, 4dc into next 4sts, 3t-ch.

Row 8: Rep Row 6.

Row 9: Skip first dc, 2dc into next 2dc, skip 2ch, 1sc, (7ch, 1sc into top of loop) four times. 7ch, 1sc into fourth ch, skip 2ch, 2dc into next 2sts, 3t–ch.

Row 10: Rep Row 6.

Row 11: Rep Row 9.

Rows 12–17: Rep Rows 6 and 9 alt.

Row 18: Skip first dc, 1dc, 3ch, skip 3ch, (4ch, 1sc into top of loop) four times. 4ch, skip 3ch, 1dc into first dc, 2dc into next 2dc, 1t–ch.

Row 19: Skip first dc (2sc into next 2sts, skip 1st), repeat to end. Fasten off.

Using yarn B put hook through first chain space (1-ch sp) made on Round 1, yoh and pull yarn through, work 3ch. (1dc, 1ch, 2dc) all in the same 1-ch space (1ch, 2dc) twice in each of next three 1–ch sps. 1ch, 1sl st in third of first 3ch. Fasten off.

Sewing up
Use yarn A, crochet hook D/3.

Pin base to front panel. Join with 1 line sc. Rep with back panel.

Pin side panel to base, join with 1 line sc. Rep with other side panel.

Pin side panels to front, join with 1 line sc. Rep all around the bag joining all the side seams.

Weave in all ends, turn inside out.

Sew buttons on to intersections in the front and back mesh randomly, 14 on each side.

Handle
Use yarn A and crochet hook D/3

Make 8ch.

Row 1: 1sc into third ch from hook, 1sc into each rem ch to end, 1t–ch. (6sts).

Row 2: Skip first sc, 1sc into each rem ch to end, 1t–ch.

Rep Row 2 138 times, fasten off.

Double up the 59in (150cm) rope/washing line, securing with tape at both ends.

Enclose rope in the crochet strip, leaving four rows free. Join crochet with 1 line sc, enclosing rope as you join.

Sew flat ends into bag.

Weave in all yarn ends.

Tie bolero

This fashionable cardigan can either be tied at the front or wrapped and tied at either the side or the back. It is made using the very soft Debbie Bliss Baby Cashmerino in a delicate but simple stitch. It is an excellent garment either for the daytime, or when you want to dress up for the evening.

MEASUREMENTS

To fit bust sizes 30/34/38in (76/86/97cm)
Chest: 32/36/41in (81/92/104cm)
Length: 16½/17½/18in (42/44/46cm)
Sleeve length: 12¼/13/13½in (31/33/34cm)

MATERIALS

Debbie Bliss Baby Cashmerino (50g balls)
shade 609, Mauve x 8/9/10 balls

Crochet hooks: size C/2, size D/3 and size E/4

GAUGE

26 stitches and 15 rows to 4in (10cm) over pattern on size E/4 crochet hook.

STITCHES USED

single crochet, slip stitch, double crochet

ABBREVIATIONS

ch chain	rep repeat
dc double crochet	sc single crochet
dec decrease	sl st slip stitch
inc increase	nxt next
alt alternate	patt pattern
RS right side	WS wrong side
foll following	tch turning chain

METHOD

12st repeat plus 1st.
Row 1: (RS) 2dc into third ch from hook, * skip 2 ch, 1 sc into nxt ch, 5ch skip 5ch, 1sc into nxt ch, skip 2ch, 5dc into nxt ch, rep from * ending last rep with only 3dc into last ch, turn.
Row 2: 1ch, 1sc into first st, *5ch, 1sc into nxt 5ch arch, 5ch, 1sc into third dc of nxt 5dc; rep from * ending last rep with 1sc into top of tch. Turn.
Row 3: *5ch, 1sc into nxt 5 arch, 5dc into nxt sc, 1sc into nxt arch, rep from * ending 2ch, 1dc into last sc, skip tch, turn.
Row 4: 1ch, 1sc into first st, *5ch, 1sc into third dc of nxt 5dc, 5ch, 1sc into nxt 5ch arch, rep from * to end, turn.
Row 5: 3ch (count as 1dc), 2dc into first st, * 1sc into nxt arch, 5ch 1sc into nxt arch, 5dc into nxt sc; rep from * ending last rep with only 3dc into last sc, skip tch, turn.
Repeat Rows 2, 3, 4 and 5.

Back

Using E/4 hook, make 111/123/135 chain (includes 2ch extra for base row).
Commence pattern by repeating the first row of the 12st pattern across base chain, turn. Do 9/10/11 repeats.
Continue working patt as set, repeating Rows 2, 3, 4 and 5.
Work till patt measures 8⅝/8¾/9½in (22/22.5/24cm), ending with RS facing for nxt row.
Shape armhole (when shaping count every ch, sc, dc as 1st).
Sl st across first 3sts, 1sc into nxt st, patt to last 4sts, 1sc into nxt st, turn.
Nxt row: Rep last row once more, turn.
Now work patt as set till armhole measures 7/7/8in (18/18/20cm). End with RS facing for nxt row.

Back neck shaping

Work three repeats of patt for size 1 and 2. Size 3 work 3.5 repeats. (37/37/43sts.) This includes first st.
Nxt row: Sl st across first 6sts, patt to end, turn.
Nxt row: Patt to end.
Nxt row: Sl st across 6sts, patt to end. Fasten off. (25/25/31 sts.)
With RS facing, skip nxt four arches. Join yarn to nxt sc, foll patt to end.
Now work neck as above but reverse shaping. Fasten off.

Left front

As before when decreasing, count every ch, sc, and dc as 1st each. Using E/4 hook, make 147/153/159 ch.
Now follow pattern repeat as set for back.12/12.5/13 patt repeats.

First and third sizes

Work two rows. RS facing for nxt row.

Second size

Row 1: Work to last rep then skip 2ch, 1sc into nxt ch, 2ch, skip 2ch, 1dc into last st, turn.
Nxt Row: Work as Row 4.

All sizes

Now continue with patt as set. Work the following shaping:
With RS facing for nxt row.
Work to last 18sts then 3dc (3dc; 2ch 1dc) into nxt sc, turn.
Nxt row: Sl st across first 18sts patt to end, turn.
Nxt row: Patt to last 18sts then work 2ch 1dc into nxt sc (5ch, 1sc into nxt arch; 2ch, 1dc into nxt sc), turn.
Nxt row: This row and 5/5/4 alternate rows, dec 6sts at inner edge, ending with WS facing for nxt row.
Nxt row: Work to end. 55/61/67sts remain.
Nxt row: This row and foll 7/9/10 alt rows, dec 3sts at inner edge, ending with WS. At same time, when having worked the same number of rows as back to armhole, start armhole shaping as follows:
RS facing.
Sl st across first 3sts, 1sc into nxt st, patt as set.
Nxt row: Patt to last 4sts, sc into nxt st, turn.
When having worked all the decreases, 25/25/31sts remain.
Continue straight until armhole measures same as back to end of back neck shaping. Fasten off.

Right front

Work same as left front reversing all shaping.

Sleeves (both alike)
First size only
Using size C/2 hook, make 63ch.

Work patt as set for back, work six rows, ending with RS facing for nxt row. Change to size E/4 hook.

Second and third sizes

Using size E/4 hook throughout, make 63/75ch.
Work six rows as set by back, ending with RS facing for nxt row.
5/5/6 patt repeats.
Now start side shaping:
Row 7 (inc row): 8ch, 1sc into first arch, *5dc into nxt sc, 1sc into nxt arch, 5ch, 1sc into nxt five arches, rep from *to last two arches then work 5dc into nxt sc, 1sc into nxt arch, 5ch, 1dc into last sc, turn.
Row 8: 1ch, 1sc into first st, 3ch, 1sc into 5ch arch, patt as Row 4 of main patt to last arch, 3ch, 1sc into same loop, turn.
Row 9: 1ch, 1sc into first st, * 5dc into nxt sc, 1sc into nxt 5ch arch, 5ch, 1sc into nxt 5ch arch, rep from * to last arch, 5dc into nxt sc, 1sc into last sc, turn.
Row 10: 1ch, 1sc into first st, 3ch, 1sc into third dc of nxt 5dc, * 5ch, 1sc into nxt 5ch arch, 5ch, 1sc into third dc of nxt 5dc, rep from * to last 5dc group, 5ch, 1sc into third dc of nxt 5dc, 2ch, 1dc into last st, turn.
Row 11 (inc row): 3ch, 2dc into first st, 1sc into 2ch arch, then patt as Row 5 of main patt to end, working 5ch, 1sc into last 3ch arch, 3dc into last st, turn.
Rows 12–14 inclusive: Work as main patt Rows 2-4.
Row 15 (inc row): Work as Row 5 of main patt but work 4dc instead of 2dc at beg of row and 5dc instead of 3dc at end of row.
Row 16: As Row 10 (above).
Row 17: Work as Row 5 of main patt, omitting first 3ch, 2dc and last 3dc, work 1ch, 1sc into first st, 5ch, 1sc into 5ch arch, work to end with 1sc into last st, turn.
Row 18: As Row 2 of main patt to last arch, work 3ch, 1sc into last st, turn.
Row 19 (inc row): Work as Row 3 of main patt but work 5ch, 1sc into first 3ch arch, work to end.
Rows 20–22 inclusive: Work Rows 4/5/2 of main patt , then rep Rows 7–19 inclusive 9/9/10 patt repeats remain.

Now work 11/13/15 rows straight, ending with RS facing for nxt row.

Shape armhole

Sl st across 3sts, 1sc into nxt st, work to last 4sts, 1sc into nxt st, turn.

Nxt row: Repeat last row once more. Fasten off.

Sewing up

Press all pieces lightly. Sew shoulder, side and sleeve seams using a flat seam stitch.

Edgings

Body

With RS facing, starting at lower left side seam, and using D/3 hook, work as follows:

Row 1: Work 1sc into foundation row, * 4ch, 1sc* (1 arch made) evenly spaced, rep from * to * along all edges, taking care not to let the arches be too deep, sl st into first sc, do not turn.

Row 2: Work 4sc into each arch end, sl st into first sc, fasten off.

Lower sleeve edging

Work the same as for body.

Fasten off.

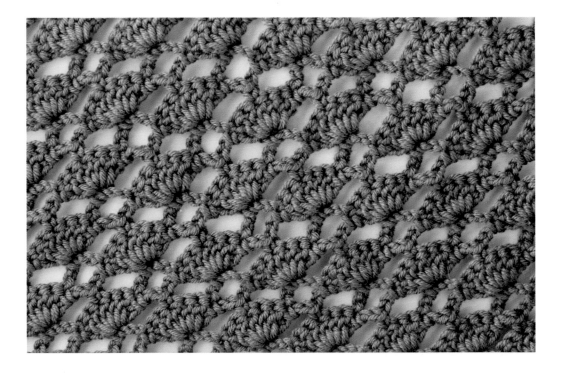

Flower-power beaded belt

This beaded belt is full of character, bright and colorful with pretty beads and an attractive bow that ties at the front or the side. Wear it with jeans or over a skirt. The flowers are a feature that make the belt a perfect accessory for any garment.

SIZES

Small: 8–12 flowers
Medium: 12–16 flowers
Large: 16–18 flowers

MATERIALS

Debbie Bliss Cotton DK (50g balls)
Choose 3 balls from the following colors:
shade 37, Lilac
shade 36, Orange
shade 35, Yellow
shade 38, Pink
shade 15, Red
shade 20, Light Green
shade 31, Purple

Crochet hook: size G/6

Approx: 94½in (2.4m) ribbon, ⅝in (15mm) wide
22 assorted beads big enough for yarn to thread through
2 beads with big enough hole for ribbon to go through

STITCHES USED

slip stitch, double crochet, double crochet two together

ABBREVIATIONS

ch chain   sc single crochet
sl st slip stitch   dc double crochet
dc2tog double crochet two together as follows over next 2sc
Yoh, insert hook into next st, yoh and pull through. Yoh, pull through two loops (leaving two loops on hook). Yoh, insert hook into next st and pull through. Yoh, pull through two loops, yoh and pull through all three loops.

METHOD

Leaving a long tail (approx 6in [15.5cm]), make 6ch, join with sl st to make a ring.

Round 1: Work 18sc into ring catching tail into chain, sl st into first sc.

Round 2: *3ch dc2tog (see abbreviations). 3ch, sl st into next sc*. Repeat * to * five more times. (Six petals). Place last sl st into last sc of previous round. Fasten off.

Pull tail from first 6ch to tighten flower hole.

Finishing
Attaching beads and flowers

1. Thread needle with same color yarn as one of the flowers.
2. Insert needle into same color flower with a secure stitch.
3. Thread one bead through needle and onto yarn. Push bead up close to flower, make a secure stitch into second flower and thread yarn back through bead to first flower, make a secure stitch and fasten off.
4. Weave in ends.

Attaching the ribbon

Cut ribbon to two lengths of 1.2m (47in) long.

1   With one piece of ribbon and belt wrong side facing, thread end of ribbon up through the gap (between the 3ch and the dc2tog) of petal opposite beads and back downwards through the gap on the adjacent petal.
2. Turn belt to right side facing. Pull ribbon through so you have two equal lengths.
3. Thread both ends of ribbon through a needle with a large eye. It's easier to fold the ribbon in half before threading through. Push needle through bead and push bead up towards flower. Trim ends of ribbon to fit so it sits close to flower just touching the edges.

Repeat on other end.

Summer brimmed hat

This is a cool and stylish way to keep the sun's rays off your face, especially when styled with your aviator sunglasses. A must-have for every conscientious girl who wants to keep the sun off; it scrunches up, easily fits into a bag and creates an ultra cool look.

MEASUREMENTS
One size: 20in (50cm)

MATERIALS
(50g balls)
Rowan Handknit Cotton
Yarn A: shade 219, Gooseberry x 1 ball
Yarn B: shade 318, Seafarer x 1 ball
Rowan Cotton Glacé
Yarn C: shade 815, Excite x 1 ball
Yarn D: shade 812, Ivy x 1 ball

Crochet hooks: size B/1 and size G/6

STITCHES USED
chain, single crochet, treble, half double crochet, double crochet, double treble, slip stitch

ABBREVIATIONS
ch chain	sc single crochet
sp space	sl st slip stitch
dc double crochet	WS wrong side
RS right side	dtr double treble
hdc half double crochet	rep repeat
tr treble	

GAUGE
6ch x 5 rows to 2in (5cm) using size G/6 hook using half double crochet.

METHOD
Using G/6 hook and yarn A make 5ch. Join with sl st to make a ring.

Round 1: Make 3 ch. Work *1hdc into circle, 1ch*. Repeat *to* six more times. Join with sl st to second of 3ch.

Round 2: Make 3ch. *1hdc 1ch 1hdc 1ch in each sp between hdcs. Repeat from * to end. Join with sl st to second of 3ch.

Round 3: Using yarn B make 3ch. 1hdc, 1ch in same ch sp *1hdc 1ch 1hdc into next ch sp. 1hdc 1ch into next ch sp*. Repeat from *to* to end. Join with sl st to second of 3ch.

Round 4: Make 3ch. Skip first sp. *work 1hdc, 1ch into next sp*. Repeat from *to* to end. Join with sl st to second of 3ch.

Round 5: Using yarn A make 3ch. 1hdc in first sp, 1ch. *1hdc 1ch twice in next sp. 1hdc 1ch into each of next 2sps*. Repeat from *to* to last sp. 1hdc 1ch. Join with sl st as before.

Round 6: As Round 4.

Round 7: Using yarn B make 3ch. Work 1hdc 1ch in first sp*. 1hdc 1ch in next 2sps. 1hdc 1ch 1hdc 1ch in next sp*. Repeat from *to* to end. Join with sl st in second of 3ch.

Rounds 8-12: As Round 4, but change yarns on Round 9 to yarn A and on Round 11 to yarn B

Rounds 13-16: As Round 4, but change yarns on Round 13 to yarn A and on Round 15 to yarn B.

Round 17: Same as Round 4, using yarn A.

Rounds 18 to 21: As Rounds 4 and 6 but change yarns on Round 19 to B and Round 21 to A.

Round 22: As Round 12.

Brim
Round 1: Using yarn B make 3ch, *2hdc in next sp six times, 1hdc in next sp*. Rep from * to * until end. Join with sl st to second of 3ch.

Round 2: Make 3ch, *1hdc in sp between hdcs four times, 2hdc in next sp*. Rep from * to * until end. Join with sl st to second of 3ch.

Round 3: Change to yarn A and work as in Round 2.

Round 4: Make 3ch. * 1hdc in each sp.* Rep from * to * until end. Join with sl st to second of 3ch.

Round 5: Change to yarn B. Make 3ch. * 1hdc in next sp nine times, 2hdcs in next sp.* Rep from * to * until end. Join with sl st to second of 3ch.

Rounds 6–9: As Round 5 but change yarn on Round 7 to yarn A and Round 9 to yarn B.

Round 10: Using two ends of yarn C make 2ch. 1sc in each sp to end. Join with sl st and fasten off.

Flowers

In yarn C, using only one end make 49ch.

Row 1: 1sc in fourth ch from hook, *2ch, skip 2ch, 1sc in next ch.* Rep to end. 1ch, turn.

Row 2: 3sc in sp four times, 4dc in next sp three times, 5dc in next sp twice, 4tr in next sp, 5tr in next sp twice, 4dtr in next sp, 5dtr in next sp twice, 3dtr in last sp.

With RS facing, and starting at the beginning of Row 2, roll up the work and sew together through the foundation chain to form a rose. To make a more open flower sew it together with WS facing.

Leaf

In yarn D make 11ch. 1sc in second ch from hook, 1sc, 1hdc, 3dc, 1hdc, 2sc, 3sc in last ch. Continue working down the other side of the foundation ch until the end. Join with a sl st. Fasten off.

Finishing

Using yarn C sew the flower on to the hat where you would like it to be placed. Using yarn D sew the leaves on to make a little posy. Neatly sew in all the yarn ends.

  *Cool Girl's Patterns... To Get You Hooked*

Daisy cashmere scarf

Making crochet squares is the perfect occupation for snatched moments, as you only make one square at a time. This crochet-square scarf is made out of Debbie Bliss Baby Cashmerino using simple crochet stitches and is beautifully soft.

MATERIALS
Debbie Bliss Baby Cashmerino (50g balls)
Yarn A (main color): shade 609, Purple x 2 balls
Yarn B: shade 600, Pink x 1 ball
Yarn C: shade 503, Green x 1 ball
Yarn D: shade 203, Teal x 1 ball

Crochet hook: size D/3

The scarf is made up of 34 squares joined together, edged with a single crochet stitch and decorated with mini pom-poms.

STITCHES USED
single crochet, double crochet, three double crochet cluster, half double crochet, slip stitch

ABBREVIATIONS
ch chain	sc single crochet
ch sp chain space	hdc half double crochet
dc double crochet	yoh yarn over hook
sp space	sl st slip stitch
RS right side	

How to make a three double crochet cluster

1. Wrap the yarn over hook (yoh), insert hook into stitch, yoh and draw through to the front, yoh and draw through two loops (two loops remain on the hook).
2. Yoh, insert hook into the stitch, yoh and draw through to the front, yoh and draw through two loops (three loops remain on the hook).
3. Repeat step 2. There will be four loops remaining on the hook.
4. Yoh and pull through all four loops. This completes your three double crochet cluster.

METHOD

Using yarn A make 6ch. Join with a sl st in first ch to form a ring.

Round 1 (RS): Using yarn A make 3ch (this counts as one double crochet). Make 1dc into the ring, *1ch, 2dc in ring*. Repeat from * to * twice more. Make 1ch, 1sl st in top of first 3ch. Fasten off.

Round 2: Using yarn B slip stitch into first chain space (ch sp), made on Round 1, make 3ch. 1dc, 1ch, 2dc all in the same ch space. 1ch, 2dc twice in each of next 3ch sps. 1ch, 1sl st in top of first 3ch. Fasten off.

Round 3: Using yarn C join with sl st in first ch sp made on Round 2. *3ch, make 1hdc into second ch sp along, 3ch, make one cluster, 4ch, 1 cluster into second ch sp along*. Repeat *to* twice until you have four corners. 3ch, make 1hdc into second ch sp along, 3ch, 1sl st into top st of first 3ch. Don't fasten off.

Round 4: Using yarn D. Join with a sl st in second ch sp made on Round 3. 3ch, make 1 cluster, make 4 ch, make 1 cluster into same ch sp. *3ch, make 1hdc into second ch sp along, 3ch, make 1 cluster, 4ch, 1 cluster into second ch sp along*. Repeat *to* twice more, until you have four corners. 3ch, make 1hdc into second ch sp along, 3ch, sl st into top st of first 3ch. Don't fasten off.

Round 5: Continue using yarn D. 1ch, *1sc in top of next 2sts. 4sc in next ch sp. 1sc into top of next 2sts. 3sc in next ch sp. 1sc in top of hdc. 3sc in next ch sp.* Repeat from * to * three more times.

Sl st into top of next st. Fasten off. Use different color combinations for each square.

Make 34 squares.

Sewing up

Place squares together in a line, two squares wide. With RS facing and using yarn A, join squares with a single crochet into each stitch, up center line (vertically), then join squares across (horizontally) so that all squares are joined together.

Edging

Use yarn A.

With RS facing, join yarn with sl st.

Make a single crochet into every stitch across top, sides and bottom of scarf until you have finished one row.

Cast off.

Neatly sew in ends.

Add some mini pom-poms (see page 33).

Attaching mini pom-poms to scarf

1. Take a piece of yarn the same color as pom-pom and join to edge of scarf.
2. Make 4ch.
3. Pick up a mini pom-pom and push hook into two of the loops that are holding the pom-pom together in its center.
4. Slip stitch to pull yarn through and cast off.
5. Break yarn and cut to blend in with pom-pom.
6. Sew in yarn ends neatly.
7. Fluff up pom-pom with a brush. Hold pom-pom very firmly and softly brush with quick sharp motion.

Attach five pom-poms to each end of the scarf.

Fingerless gloves

These fingerless gloves, a mixture of Debbie Bliss Alpaca and Silk, are the height of luxury and indulgence. They are very simple to make and elegant and comfortable to wear. Crocheted in the round, the ruffle and the thumbhole are the last parts to be made. The thumbhole is formed by Rounds 22–23.

MATERIALS
Debbie Bliss Alpaca Silk DK (50g balls)
shade 12, Green x 2 balls

Crochet hook: size F/5

STITCHES USED
chain stitch, single crochet, slip stitch, double crochet, treble

ABBREVIATIONS
ch chain stitch	st stitch
sts stitches	sc single crochet
dc double crochet	tr treble
sl st slip stitch	

METHOD
Make 36ch, join into a round using a sl st.

Round 1: 1ch, skip first st, 1sc in each remaining st in round, ending with a sl st into first st.
Round 2: 6ch, skip 3sts, 1dc, * 3ch, skip 3sts, 1dc. Repeat from * seven times. 3ch, sl st into third of first 6ch in round.
Round 3: 1ch, skip first st, 1sc into each remaining st in round, finish round with a sl st into the first st.
Rounds 4–9: As Round 3.
Round 10: 1ch, skip first st, 4sc, * skip next st, 4sc, Repeat from * to end of round, ending with a sl st.
Round 11: 1ch, skip first st, 1sc into each remaining st in round, ending with a sl st.
Round 12: 1ch, skip first st, * 3 sc, 2sc into next st. Repeat from * to end of round, ending with a sl st.

Rounds 13–21: As Round 3.
Round 22: Left glove: 1ch, skip first st, 2sc, 5ch, skip 5 sts, 1sc into next st, 1sc into each remaining st in round, ending with 1sl st. (For right glove: 1ch, skip first st, 1sc into each st until last 7sts, 5ch, skip 5sts, 1sc into next st, 1sc into next st, sl st.)
Round 23: 1ch, skip first st, 1 sc into each st in round (including 5ch sts of previous round). Ending with a sl st.
Rounds 24–26: As Round 3.
Round 27: 1ch, skip first st, 8sc, skip next st, 8sc, skip next st, 8sc, skip next st, 1sc into each remaining st, ending with a sl st.
Rounds 28–30: As Round 3.
Round 31: *5ch, skip 3 sts, 1sc into next st. Repeat from * to end.
Round 32: *5ch, 1sc into third ch of first 5ch loop, Repeat from * to end.
Round 33: As Round 32, fasten off last st.

Thumb
Rejoin yarn to thumbhole created by Rounds 22–23.
Round 1: 1sc into each of 5sts at top of hole and follow round to 1sc in each of 5sts at bottom of thumbhole, join to first st with 1sl st.
Round 2: 1ch, skip first st, 1sc into each st, join with a sl st.
Rounds 3–5: As Round 2.
Fasten off.

Ruffle
Join yarn onto first dc st, at wrist end of glove.
*Make 7tr along this st (around the stitch itself, not into it).
1tr into second of 3sts at base of st.
Make 7tr along next dc st (around the stitch itself, not into it).
1tr into second of 3sts at top of st.* Repeat until the ruffle meets up around wrist. Join together with 1sl st.
Fasten off.

Cool Girl's Patterns... To Get You Hooked

Beaded purse

Beaded crochet is at the height of fashion, seen accompanying the most high-profile of couture on the catwalks. This pretty purse has delicate pearl beads and a pull-string tie.

MATERIALS
Rooster Almerino Aran (50g balls)
Yarn A: shade 301, Cornish x 1 ball
Yarn B: shade 307, Brighton Rock x 1 ball
Approx 100 Pearl White Mill Hill Glass pebble beads

Crochet hook size D/3

STITCHES USED
single crochet, slip stitch, double crochet, treble

ABBREVIATIONS
ch chain   inc increase
sl st slip stitch   sc single crochet
tr treble   dc double crochet

METHOD
All stitches are worked into the back of the stitch to create a ridge.

Using yarn A make 4ch. Join with a sl st in first ch to form a ring. After each round, join with a sl st.

Round 1: Work 8sc into ring.
Round 2: (1sc, inc in next st) four times (12sts).
Round 3: (1sc, inc in next st) six times (18sts).
Round 4: (1sc, inc in next st) nine times (27sts).
Round 5: (2sc, inc in next st) nine times (36sts).
Round 6: 1sc into each st (36sts).
Round 7: (3sc, inc in next st) nine times (45sts).
Round 8: 1sc into each st (45sts).
Round 9: (4sc, inc in next st) nine times (54sts).
Round 10: 1sc into each st (54sts).
Round 11: (5sc, inc in next st) nine times (63sts).

Round 12: 1sc into each st (63sts).
Round 13: Tr into each st (63sts).
Round 14: *1ch, insert bead, 1sc into every other st* (63sts).
Round 15: 1dc into each st (63sts).
Round 16: 1sc into each st (63sts).
Round 17: *tr into each st, insert bead every other tr* (63sts).
Round 18: 1sc into each st (63sts).
Round 19: *1ch, tr into every other st* (63sts).
Round 20: 1sc into every st (63sts).
Round 21: 1dc into every st (63sts).
Round 22: *1sc into every st, insert bead every other sc* (63sts).
Round 23: *1ch, tr into every other st* (63sts).
Round 24: 1sc into every st (63sts).
Round 25: 1dc into every st (63sts).
Round 26: *1ch, 1dc into every other st* (63sts).
Round 27: Tr into every st (63sts).
Round 28: *1ch, 1dc into every other st* (63sts).
Round 29: Tr into every st (63sts).
Round 30: *1ch, 1dc into every other st * (62sts), Fasten off.

Handle
The handle is made by creating a long ribbon, which is threaded through Round 27 of the purse.
Using yarn B make a 200ch.
Insert hook into third chain from hook. Work 197dc into chain. Fasten off.

Picot edge
Using yarn B
1sl st into first st, (5ch, sl st into third ch from hook, 2ch, skip 2st, 1sl st into next st) repeat to end, fasten off.

Ribbon slippers

Cosy, cute, and very sought after, in recent trends crochet slippers have been a key item in fashionable shops. Everyone will be envious of these beautiful handmade slippers with a pretty flower and ribbon.

MEASUREMENTS

Small size approximately size 2.5–4.5

Medium size approximately size 4.5–5.5

Large size approximately size 6.5–7.5

MATERIALS

(50g balls)

For slippers:

Debbie Bliss Cashmerino Chunky, shade 11 x 2 balls

2m (78in) of 10mm (⅜in) wide ribbon

For flower:

Oddments of yarn or x 1 ball each of Debbie Bliss Merino DK shade 700, Red and shade 703, Pink

Crochet hooks: size G/6 for slippers; size D/3 for flower motif

STITCHES USED

single crochet, half double crochet, slip stitch, double crochet, double crochet two together

ABBREVIATIONS

ch chain	sc single crochet
hdc half double crochet	RS right side facing
sl st slip stitch	sts stitches
dc double crochet	dc2tog double crochet two together

dec decrease: *insert hook into next st, pull loop through, repeat from * once, yoh and pull through all three loops (this decreases 1 stitch).

Tip: Dc2tog work 1dc into each of next 2sc. Yoh, insert hook into next sc, draw yarn through, yoh and draw through two loops on hook (two loops remain). Yoh, insert hook into next sc, draw yarn through, yoh and draw through two loops on hook (three loops remain). Yoh and draw through the three loops on hook. Yoh wrap yarn over hook.

METHOD

Soles

Make 20/24/28 ch (3 sizes).

Row 1: Work 2hdc into second ch from hook, 2hdc into next ch, 1hdc into each of next 15/19/23ch, 2hdc into next ch, 3hdc into last chain. Working into other side of chain, work 2hdc into next ch, 1hdc in each of the next 15/19/23sts. 2hdc in next st, 1hdc into first ch sp at beginning of work. With sl st join into top of first hdc.

Row 2: Work 2ch (counts as 1hdc), 1hdc in same space, 2hdc into each of the next 2sts, 1hdc into each of next 4sts. 1sc in each of next 11/15/19sts, 1hdc in each of next 2sts, 2hdc in each of next 5sts, 1hdc in each of next 2sts, 1sc in each of next 11/15/19sts, 1 hdc in each of next 4sts, 2 hdc in each of next 2sts. Join with sl st into top of second ch.

Row 3: Work 3ch, 1dc into same sp. 2dc in each of next 4sts, 1dc into next st, 1hdc into next 7/9/11sts. 1sc in each of next 11/13/15sts, *2sc into next st, 1sc into next st, Repeat from * once. *1sc into next st, 2sc into next st. Repeat from * once. 1sc into each of the next 11/13/15sts, 1 hdc into each of next 7/9/11sts. 1dc into next st, 2dc in each of the next 3sts. Join with a sl st into top of 3ch.

Row 4: Work 2ch, 1hdc in same space, 2hdc in each of next 6sts. 1hdc in each of next 4 sts, 1sc in each of next 21/25/29sts. 2sc in each of next 6sts, 1sc in each of next 21/25/29sts, 1hdc in each of next 4sts, 2hdc in each remaining sts. Join to first st and fasten off.

Make three more soles as above.

Upper slipper

With RS of sole facing, join yarn in any stitch at heel. Working in the back loop of stitches throughout.

Round 1: Put in a round marker and join yarn slightly to the right or left of center. 1sc in each stitch of round. Join with sl st.

Round 2: Take out round marker and place a different colored marker at the center of the toe and another at the center of the heel. 1sc into each st, until 3sts from the center of the toe. Dec 3sts (see Tip). Continue 1sc into each st until 3sts from the center marker of the heel.

Round 3: Dec 3sts. 1sc into each st until 4sts from the center marker of the toe. Dec 2sts, 1sc, dec 2sts. 1sc into each st until marker of heel.

Round 4: 1sc into each st until approximately halfway down the side between the toe and heel (instep), dec 1st. Place a marker. Continue 1sc into each st until the toe marker. Dec 1st at center of toe. Continue 1sc in each st until approximately in center of heel and toe, opposite where marker for instep has been placed. Dec 1st. Take instep marker out. Continue 1sc in each st until heel marker.

Round 5: Work 1sc into to each st until 3sts from toe marker. Dec 3sts . Continue 1sc in each st until heel marker.

Round 6: Work 1sc into each st until 4sts from toe marker. Dec 2sts, 1sc, dec 2sts. Continue 1sc in each st until 1st before heel marker.

Round 7: Dec 1st at heel. Continue 1sc in each st until 4sts before center of toe marker. Dec 2sts, 1sc, dec 2sts. Continue 1sc in each st until heel marker.

Round 8: 1sc into each st until 6sts before center of toe marker. Dec 2sts *insert hook into next st, pull loop through, repeat three times from *, yoh, pull through all loops at one time, dec 2sts. 1sc in each remaining st until 2sts before heel marker, sl st into the next 2sts to even the round.

Round 9: 3ch, skip 1st, 1hdc in next st, *1ch, skip 1st, 1hdc in next st, repeat from * until end of round. 1ch, join with sl st into top of third chain. Fasten off.

Flower

Make 6ch, join with sl st to form a ring.

Round 1: 1ch, work 15sc into ring, sl st into first sc.

Round 2: *3ch dc2tog (see Tip opposite) over next 2sc. 3ch, sl st into next sc*. Repeat * to * four more times (five petals). Place last sl st into last sc of previous round. Fasten off.

Round 3: Using yarn C, join with 1sl st in any stitch of one of the petals. *1ch, work 1sc into top of next st *, rep from * to * until end.

Pull tail from first 6ch to tighten flower hole.

Sew in ends.

Finishing

Stitch one sole onto bottom of each slipper, so that slipper is strengthened by having two soles.

Thread ribbon through loop holes and tie with a bow at the back.

Attach the flower at the front.

Hot-water bottle cover

Toasty warm, this hot-water bottle cover is made with superchunky Rowan Big Wool in soft, cosy colors. It's too good to put under the covers and needs to be shown off!

MEASUREMENTS
To fit an average sized hot-water bottle: 10¼in (26cm) width x 14½in (37cm) depth (includes top gathering).

MATERIALS
Rowan Big Wool (100g balls)
shade 029, Pistachio x 2 balls
shade 014, Whoosh x 2 balls
shade 001, White Hot x 1 ball

Crochet hook: size I/9

GAUGE
11sc stitches and 13 rows to 4in (10cm) on size I/9 crochet hook (or hook size to achieve correct gauge).

STITCHES USED
single crochet, slip stitch

ABBREVIATIONS
ch chain	sc single crochet
RS right side	nxt next
foll following	sl st slip stitch

METHOD
Front and back (both alike)
Using I/9 hook and yarn color Whoosh (pink), make 29ch. Work 1sc into second ch from hook, then 1sc into each ch to end, turn. Do not fasten off.
Next row: Change to color Pistachio (pale green), work 1ch,*1sc* into each sc to end. Turn, do not fasten off. Change to color White Hot, work one row as last row. Keeping the repeat as set, carry each yarn not in use up the side of the work, work a total of 40 rows.

With RS facing work eyelet row, keeping color repeat as set throughout, as follows:
1sc, * 1ch, skip 1ch, 1sc into nxt 2sc, rep from * to end, turn.
Next row: Work one row of scs working 1sc into each 1ch space. Work a further four rows of sc.
Fasten off.

Finishing
Sew both side seams using a flat seam stitch, leaving top open. With RS facing and using Whoosh, using size I/9 crochet hook, work picot edging as follows:
Starting at top side seam, sl st into sc of previous row, 1ch, 1sc into nxt 2sc * make picot by working 3ch, sl st into third ch from hook, skip 1sc, 1sc into nxt 3sc, rep from * to last 3sc, 1 picot, skip 1sc, 1sc into last st, sl st into first sc, fasten off.

Using a length of each color yarn, make a plait 57in (145cm) long, leaving a length of 4in (10cm) of each color at each end of plait (use these three lengths to tie the pom-poms onto each end of the plait). Thread plait through the eyelets so that each end finishes in middle of front of cover.

Pom-poms (make 2)
Cut two circles of card measuring 2in (5cm). Mark out a smaller circle in the middle of each card, cut out.
Using the three colors separately, wrap yarn around the two cards together until it is tightly packed with yarn.
With a pair of narrow-ended scissors, cut between the two cards, slightly part the cards and using the loosed ends of each plait, tie into the center of the pom-pom. Pull tightly and knot. Ease off both pieces of card and fluff up the pom-pom, trimming the outer edges to form a smooth ball. Repeat for the second pom-pom.

When the hot-water bottle is in its cover, pull the ties and make a bow to form a fit around the neck of the bottle.

Cushion cake

This cushion cover is made of two identical pieces of crochet attached together. The yarn is soft and luxurious. The edging uses a fuchsia pink from the Debbie Bliss Cashmerino Aran range that gives it a touch of glamor and the little flower adds a splash of contrasting color. It looks good enough to eat.

MEASUREMENTS
Makes cushion cover to fit a 16in (40.6cm) round cushion pad

MATERIALS
(50g balls)

Yarn A (main color): Rooster Almerino Aran, shade 301, Cornish x 3 balls

Yarn B (edging): Debbie Bliss Cashmerino Aran, shade 616, Fuchsia x 1 ball

Yarn C (flower): Debbie Bliss Alpaca Silk DK, shade 012, Green x 1 ball (alternatively, use oddments)

Yarn D (flower): Rooster Almerino Aran, shade 307, Brighton Rock x 1 ball (alternatively, use oddments)

Crochet hooks: size H/8 and size D/3

STITCHES USED
single crochet, half double crochet, slip stitch, double crochet, double crochet two together

ABBREVIATIONS

ch chain	ch chain space
sc single crochet	hdc half double crochet
MC main color	rem remaining
RS right side facing	sl st slip stitch
dc2tog double crochet two together	dc double crochet

Tip: Dc2tog as follows over next 2sc. Yoh, insert hook into next st, yoh and pull through. Yoh, pull through two loops (leaving two loops on hook). Yoh insert hook into next st and pull through. Yoh, pull through two loops, yoh and pull through all three loops.

METHOD
The number of rounds you need to make to cover your cushion will depend on your gauge. You may need to make one round less. Measure your work against your cushion pad when nearing the end.

Front and back (both alike)
Don't turn at end of rounds, work with RS facing.
Use MC (yarn A) and hook size H/8 make 4ch and join with a sl st in first ch to form a ring.

Round 1 (RS): 3ch (these 3ch at the beginning of rounds count as the first dc), make 11dc in ring, 1sl st in third of first 3dc.

Round 2: 3ch, 1dc in same st as sl st, 2dc in each of rem dc, 1sl st in third of first 3ch. (24sts)

Round 3: 3ch, 1dc in same place as sl st, *1dc in next dc, 2dc in each of next 2dc; rep from *to last 2dc, 1dc in next dc, 2dc in last dc, 1sl st in third of first 3ch. (40sts)

Round 4: 3ch, 1dc in same place as sl st, *1dc in each of next 3dc, 2dc in next dc; rep from * to last 3dc, 1dc in each of last 3dc, 1sl st in third of first 3ch. (50sts)

Round 5: 3ch, 1dc in same place as sl st. *1dc in each of next 4dc, 2dc in next dc; rep from * to last 4dc, 1dc in each of last 4dc, 1sl st in third of first 3ch. (60sts)

Round 6: 3ch, 1dc in same place as sl st, *1dc in each of next 5dc, 2dc in next dc; rep from * to last 5dc, 1dc in each of last 5dc, 1sl st in third of first 3ch. (70sts)

Round 7: 3ch, 1dc in same place as sl st, * 1dc in each of next 6dc, 2dc in next dc; rep from * to last 6dc, 1dc in each of last 6dc, 1sl st in third of first 3ch. (80sts)

Round 8: 3ch, 1dc in same place as sl st, *1dc in each of next 7dc, 2dc in next dc; rep from * to last 7dc, 1dc in each of last 7dc, 1sl st in third of first 3ch. (90sts)

Round 9: 3ch, 1dc in same place as sl st, *1dc in each of next 8dc, 2dc in next dc. Rep from *to last 8dc, 1dc in each of last 8dc, 1sl st in third of first 3ch. (100sts)

Round 10: As Round 5. (120sts)

Round 11: 3ch, 1dc in same place as sl st, *1dc in each of next 11dc, 2dc in next dc; rep from * to last 11dc, 1dc in each of last 11dc, 1sl st in third of first 3ch. (130sts)

Round 12: 3ch, 1dc in same place as sl st, *1dc in each of next 12dc, 2dc in next dc; rep from * to last 12dc, 1dc in each of last 12dc, 1sl st in third of first 3ch. (140sts)

Round 13: As Round 7. (160sts)

Round 14: 3ch, 1dc in same place as sl st, *1dc in each of next 15dc, 2dc in next dc; rep from * to last 15dc, 1dc in each of last 15dc, 1sl st in third of first 3ch. (170sts)

Fasten off.

Sew in ends.

Sewing up

With wrong sides facing each other, join using a single crochet seam (see page 29). Insert the cushion pad halfway round. Finish the single crochet seam with the cushion inside. Fasten off. Puff up cushion into shape.

Edging

The pattern for this stitch works in sections of 8sts. So you need enough stitches to divide equally by eight. To make sure you have 176sts, you will need to increase a total amount of 6sts in next round. Count your stitches at this point and if you have the incorrect amount of stitches, decrease or increase to make sure you have enough to be divided by 8.

Round 1: Using yarn B and hook size H/8, insert hook into first stitch, join yarn with a sl st. Make 1inc at beginning of round by making 2sc into next st. *Make 1sc into next 27sts. Make 2sc into next st* Repeat four times, 1sc into each st until end (176sts).

Round 2: *1ch, skip 1st, 1sc 1ch 1hdc in next st, skip 1st, 1dc 1ch 1dc in next st, skip 1st, 1hdc 1ch 1sc in next st, 1ch, skip 1st, 1sl st in next st, rep from * to end placing the last sl st in beg of round.

Round 3: *1sc, 1hdc in next ch sp, 3dc in next ch sp, 3tr 1ch 3tr in next ch sp, 3dc in next ch sp, 1hdc 1sc in next ch sp, 1sl st on sl st, rep from * to end. Fasten off.

Flower motif (make two)

With hook size 5.0mm and leaving along tail approx 15.5cm (6in), make 6ch, and join with a sl st to make a ring.

Round 1: Using yarn C, work 15sc into ring catching tail into sts, sl st into first sc.

Round 2: *3ch dc2tog (see Tip) over next 2sc. 3ch, sl st into next sc*. Repeat *to* four more times (five petals). Sl st into first sc of previous round.

Round 3: using hook size D/3, *1ch, 1sc into next st*. Rep from *to* until end. Sl st into first chain. Fasten off.
Repeat Rounds 1 and 2 to make second flower using yarn D and hook size D/3.

Thread a tapestry needle and weave in and out of stitches in center of small flower, pull gently to close up hole. Sew small flower onto bigger flower to make a double flower. Thread a yarn sewing needle with yarn and sew double flower into center of cushion. Weave in yarn ends.

Loopy cushion

Rooster Almerino Aran is the perfect yarn for this cushion; it's made with an equal mix of baby alpaca and merino wool, so it's hard to find anything softer. It is also a beautifully designed cushion, so when displayed in the corner of the sofa or on a comfy chair it will be the envy of everyone who sees it.

MEASUREMENTS

Cushion size 15½ x 15½in (40 x 40cm)

MATERIALS

Rooster Almerino Aran (50g balls)
Yarn A: shade 307, Brighton Rock x 2 balls
Yarn B: shade 308, Spiced Plum x 5 balls
Yarn C: shade 310, Rooster x 2 balls
Yarn D: shade 303, Strawberry Cream x 2 balls
Yarn E: shade 306, Gooseberry x 5 balls
Strip of card measuring ¾ x 17in (2.1 x 43cm)
4 wooden toggle buttons

Crochet hook size H/8

STITCHES USED

chain stitch, single crochet, loop stitch, slip stitch

ABBREVIATIONS

ch chain   sc single crochet
yoh yarn over hook   sl st slip stitch
RS right side

METHOD

Front piece

Make 61ch using yarn A.

Row 1: Work one row sc.

Row 2 (RS): Work one row sc.

Row 3: (Loop stitch) Insert hook into first st. *pass yarn around piece of card, yoh, draw through two loops, insert hook into next st.* Repeat along row, these loops are formed on the back of the work, pull out strip of card.

Row 4: Work one row sc.

Row 5: Change to yarn B. Work loop st row as Row 3.

Row 6: Work one row sc.

Row 7: Change to yarn C. Work loop st row as Row 3.

Row 8: Work one row sc.

Row 9: Change to yarn D. Work one row sc.

Row10: Work one row sc.

Row 11: Change to yarn E. Work loop st row as Row 3.

Row 12: Work one row sc.

Row 13: Change to yarn A. Work loop st row as Row 3.

Row 14: Work one row sc.

Row 15: Change to yarn B. Work one row sc.

Row 16: Work one row sc.

Row 17: Change to yarn C. Work loop st row as Row 3.

Row 18: Work one row sc.

Row 19: Change to yarn D. Work loop st row as Row 3.

Row 20: Work one row sc.

Row 21: Change to yarn E. Work one row sc.

Row 22: Work one row sc.

Row 23: Change to yarn A, Work loop st row as Row 3.

Row 24: Work one row sc.

Row 25: Change to yarn E. Work loop st row as Row 3.

Row 26: Work one row sc.

Row 27: Work one row sc.

Row 28: Work one row sc.

Row 29: Work loop st row as Row 3.

Row 30: Work one row sc.

Row 31: Work loop st row as Row 3.

Row 32: Work one row sc.

Repeat Rows 27 through to 32 until work measures 16½in (42cm), fasten off.

Back piece
Make 61ch using yarn E.

Row 1: Work one row sc.

Row 2: Work one row sc.

Continue in sc until work measures 13½in (34cm) all in yarn E. Fasten off.

Back overlapping flap
Make 61ch using yarn A.

Rows 1–4: Using yarn A, work sc.

Rows 5–6: Using yarn B, work sc.

Rows 7–8: Using yarn C, work sc.

Rows 9–10: Using yarn D, work sc.

Rows 11–12: Using yarn E, work sc.

Rows 13–14: Using yarn A, work sc.

Rows 15–16: Using yarn B, work sc.

Rows 17–18: Using yarn C, work sc.

Rows 19–20: Using yarn D, work sc.

Rows 21–22: Using yarn E, work sc.

Rows 23–24: Using yarn A, work sc. Fasten off.

Buttonholes formed using ch st, continue using yarn A. Rejoin yarn 11sts from edge, 7ch, skip 1sc, 1sl st into next sc. Fasten off. *skip 8sts and rejoin yarn again. 7ch, skip 1sc, 1sl st into next sc, fasten off.* Repeat from * until four buttonhole loops have been formed.
Sew in all yarn ends.

Finishing
Sew the beginning edges of cushion front and the back overlapping flap together, (both made in yarn color A) using yarn A.

To opposite end of cushion front sew on back piece edge using yarn E.

Now fold the pieces over so the left and right edges of cushion line up. The sides should be sewn up using yarn E. Ensure all colors meet up and pin pieces in place before sewing up. Where back piece and back overlapping flap meet, make sure the stripy overlapping edge is on the front outside edge of cushion and the back piece overlaps on the inside.

When all pieces are sewn together securely insert cushion through opening formed where overlapping flap lays over the back piece. When the cushion is inside, sew on the buttons to match up with the buttonhole loops on flap edge.

Clutch bag with bow

Choosing the color for this clutch bag can define it either as an elegant and sophisticated accessory, or a bright, fun bag for make-up, jewelry, or any of those other vital items a girl has to carry in her bag.

MATERIALS
(1 x 50g ball of each color)
Bag 1 (main picture): Debbie Bliss Cotton DK, shade 24, Pink (main color), shade 25, Plum (bow)
Bag 2: (this page) Rowan Handknit Cotton, shade 320, Buttercup (main color), shade 319, Mango Fool (stripe and bow)
Snap fastener (popper)

Crochet hook: size F/5

STITCHES USED
chain, single crochet, slip stitch

ABBREVIATIONS

ch chain	ch sp chain space
sc single crochet	dec decrease
ch sp chain space	rep Repeat
RS right side	sl st slip stitch
sp space	yoh yarn over hook
WS wrong side	

METHOD
Make 50ch. *Make 1 extra ch, turn, 1 sc into next ch. Make 1sc into each of the remaining 49ch until the end of the row*. *Repeat from * to * until your square measures 10in (25.5cm).

Shaping the flap
For the next 16 rows dec 1st at the beginning and end of each row. (To decrease: 1ch, insert hook into first sc, yoh and pull through, insert hook into next sc, yoh and pull through, yoh and pull through all the stitches on hook.) Fasten off.
Sew in yarn ends.

Lining the bag
After choosing a lining fabric, place your crochet onto it flat and pin into place. Make sure you have an extra ½–¾in (1.5–2cm) around the edge for a hem. Mark the outline and cut the fabric out. After removing from the crochet, fold and pin hem and hand or machine sew down. The lining should be either the same size or slightly smaller than the crochet. With WS together, pin lining onto crochet. Machine or hand sew into place. Fold bag so that the bottom edge meets the row before the flap shaping begins. Pin. Sew down both folded edges of bag leaving the top open for access.

Making the bow
Make 26ch. *Make 1sc into the next st*. Rep from * to * another 25 times. This forms a row. Rep this row 16 times. Fasten off. You should now have a rectangle of crochet.
To shape the bow, fold the square in half to locate the center. Using a leftover end of the same color yarn, fasten at the top. Make a long running stitch from center top to center bottom. Pull end, gathering at center and fasten off. You should now have a bow shape. Choose a piece of thin colored ribbon to tie around the center to cover gathering. Attach at the back. Now stitch the bow on to center bottom edge of bag flap.

Attach a snap fastener (popper) to secure flap to bag.

Placemat and coaster

A strong double knit cotton was used for this placemat and coaster, but any material works well depending on the look you want for your table. Alternative materials you can use are string, raffia or leather–in such cases use the same pattern but change the size of the hook accordingly.

MATERIALS

(50g balls)

Yarn A: Rowan Handknit Cotton DK, shade 252, Black x 2 balls

Yarn B: Debbie Bliss Cotton DK, shade 29, Blue x 2 balls

Yarn C: Rowan Handknit Cotton DK, shade 205, Linen x 2 balls

Crochet hook size: H/8

STITCHES USED

single crochet, slip stitch

ABBREVIATIONS

ch chain

sl st slip stitch

sc single crochet

inc increase

METHOD

Placemat

Using yarn A make 4ch. Join with a sl st in first ch to form a ring

Work in a spiral as follows marking rounds as you go.

Round 1: work 8sc into ring.

Round 2: (1sc, inc in next sc) four times. (12sts)

Round 3: (1sc, inc in next sc) six times. (18sts)

Round 4: Change to yarn B, (1sc, inc in next sc) nine times. (27sts)

Round 5: (2sc, inc in next sc) nine times. (36sts)

Round 6: Change to yarn C, 1sc into each sc. (36sts)

Round 7: (3sc, inc in next sc) nine times. (45sts)

Round 8: Change to yarn A, 1sc into each sc. (45sts)

Round 9: Change to yarn C, (4sc, inc in next sc) nine times. (54sts)

Round 10: 1sc into each sc. (54sts)

Round 11: Change to yarn B (5sc, inc in next sc) nine times. (63sts)

Round 12: 1sc into each sc. (63sts)

Round 13: (3sc, inc in next sc, 3sc) nine times. (72sts)

Round 14: Change to yarn A (7sc, inc in next sc) nine times. (81sts)

Round 15: 1sl st into each sc, fasten off.

Weave in all yarn ends and steam flat.

Coaster

Using yarn A make 4ch. Join with a sl st in first ch to form a ring

Round 1: work 8sc into ring.

Round 2: (1sc, inc in next sc) four times. (12sts)

Round 3: Change to yarn B (1sc, inc in next sc) six times. (18sts)

Round 4: (1sc, inc in next sc) nine times. (27sts)

Round 5: Change to yarn C (2sc, inc in next sc) nine times. (36sts)

Round 6: Change to yarn B 1sc into each sc. (36sts)

Round 7: Change to yarn A (3sc, inc in next sc) nine times. (45sts)

Round 8: 1sl st into each sc, fasten off.

Weave in ends and steam flat.

Love Questionnaire

1. **What do you wear when you're trying to attract the opposite sex?**
   a. Full evening dress with high heels
   b. Sexy miniskirt and a boob tube
   c. A hip skinny crocheted stripy scarf worn with a denim skirt and big boots

2. **On your first date where would you go?**
   a. To the cinema
   b. To a club
   c. Knit/Crochet club night/Stitch 'n Bitch group

3. **What tickets would you like to be given for your first date with a new man?**
   a. Green Day gig
   b. Popular Broadway show
   c. As an audience member of a Craft TV network, where you participate in a crochet circle full of men and women who crochet

4. **Where would you go for a weekend away with your honey?**
   a. 5-star hotel with spa
   b Somewhere in the North in a log cabin
   c. Visit a sheep farm in northern Scotland where they spin their own fleece from the underbelly of a sheep that eats seaweed

5. **What's your favorite swimwear your partner wears?**
   a. Surf shorts/bikini
   b. Speedos
   c. Crocheted cotton swimming trunks/bikini in the latest colors

6. **On a date which sporting event would you prefer to be taken to?**
   a. Football
   b. Baseball
   c. The world's fastest crochet competition

7. **On a cosy night in with your partner would you prefer?**
   a. To snuggle up on the sofa listening to music
   b. Eat a TV dinner and a bag of popcorn
   c. Do a joint crochet project where you crochet each other a beanie hat

8. **What do you look for in a partner?**
   a. Beautiful eyes
   b., Good personality
   c. Strong arms to hold up your hanks of wool, while you wind it into a ball

ANSWERS:

Mostly a's:
You take life too seriously. Go straight to your computer, go online and find your nearest Knit/Crochet group and join immediately.

Mostly b's:
You're in danger of letting life pass you by, You'll never find a partner if you continue in this way. You need to crochet more, go and buy some needles and yarn and make the scarf on page 73.

Mostly c's:
What a wonderful person you are. You must attract potential partners every time you set your crocheted slipper outside the door.

★ Stockists

USA

Anny Blatt USA
7796 Boardwalk
Brighton, MI 48116
e: info@annyblattusa.com
w: annyblatt.com
t: 248 486 6160

Blue Sky Alpacas, Inc
PO Box 387
St. Francis, MN 55070
t: 763 753 5815
w: blueskyalpacas.com
e: sylvia@blueskyalpacas.com

Knit Café
8441 Melrose Avenue
Los Angeles
CA 90069
t: 323 658 5648
e: knitcafe@aol.com
w: knitcafe.com

The Knitting Garden
25 Long Meadow Road
Uxbridge
MA 01569
t: 888 381 9276
e: elizabether@
    theknittinggarden.com
w: theknittinggarden.com

Knitting Fever Inc
35 Debevoise Avenue
Roosevelt
NY 11575
w: knittingfever.com

Lion Brand Yarns
34 W. 15th St.
New York, NY 10011
t: 800 258 YARN (9276)
w: lionbrand.com

Purl
137 Sullivan Street
New York
NY 10012
t: 212 420 8796
e: customerservice@purlsoho.com
w: store.purlsoho.com

Zecca (clay buttons)
P.O. Box 1664 Lakeville
CT 06039
t: 860-435-2211
w: zecca.net
karen@zecca.net

UK

Colinette Yarns Ltd
Banwy Workshops
Llanfair Caereinion
Powys
Wales SY21 0SG, UK
t: 00 44 (0)1938 810128
e: info@colinette.com
w: colinette.com

Designer Yarns
Unit 8-10
Newbridge Industrial Estate
Pitt Street
Keighley
W Yorkshire BD21 4PQ, UK
t: 00 44 (0)1535 664222
e: jane@designeryarns.uk.com
w: .designeryarns.uk.com

Injabulo Buttons
Broom Cottage
Ashton
Oundle
Peterborough PE8 5LD
t: 01832 274881
e: info@injabulo.com
w: injabulo.com

Laughing Hens
Southover Nurseries
Spring Lane
Burwash
East Sussex TN19 7JB, UK
t: 00 44 (0)1435 884010
e: info@laughinghens.com
w: laughinghens.com

Rooster Yarns
Southover Nurseries
Spring Lane
Burwash
East Sussex TN19 7JB, UK
t: 00 44 (0)1435 884010
e: info@roosteryarns.com
w: roosteryarns.com

Rowan Yarns
Green Lane Mill
Holmfirth
HD9 2DX, UK
t: 0044 (0)1484 681881
w: .knitrowan.co.uk

Vogue Crochet Hooks
t: 0044 (0)208 510 9941
e: akgunlu@msn.com
w: diktex.com

★ Useful addresses

Cast Off
w: castoff.info
e: info@castoff.info

Crochet Guild of America
1100-H Brandywine Blvd
Zanesville, OH 43701-7303
w: crochet.org
e: CGOA@crochet.org
t: 740 452 4541

Craft Yarn Council of America
PO Box 9
Gastonia, NC 28053

w: craftyarncouncil.com
e: info@craftyarncouncil.com
t: 704 824 7838

The Warm Up America Foundation
w: warmupamerica.com
e: info@warmupamerica.org

Yarn Standards
w: YarnStandards.com
e: cycainfo@aol.com

WEBSITES

There are a feast of amazing and interesting crochet websites. The following websites were relevant at the time of press. If they are no longer there, just type in 'crochet' into a search engine and all sorts of interesting sites appear and lure you into the world of crochet.

Crochet Couture:	http://www.anacam.com/hats/
Crochet for men:	http://crochetformen.blogmatrix.com/
Crochet Sculpture:	http://mysung.tripod.com/artscape.html
Knitting Magazine:	www.knitty.com
Not Your Granny's	http://crochet.nearlythere.com/cgi-bin/
Crochet:	wiki.cgi/Not_Your_Granny's_Crochet

★ Index